Common Errors and Problems in English

Robert Allen is an experienced lexicographer and writer on a wide range of language topics. He edited the Pocket Oxford edition of *Fowler's Modern English Usage*, contributed to the *Oxford Companion to the English Language* and the *Oxford History of English Lexicography*, and is editor-in-chief of the *Penguin English Dictionary*. He has written another volume in this series of Writers' Guides, *How to Write Better English*, and has also written for Penguin the highly acclaimed *Allen's Dictionary of English Phrases*. Robert Allen lives in Edinburgh.

The Penguin Writers' Guides

PENGUIN WRITERS' GUIDES

Common Errors and Problems in English

ROBERT ALLEN

PENGUIN BOOKS

PENGUIN BOOKS

Published by the Penguin Group
Penguin Books Ltd, 80 Strand, London WC2R 0RL, England
Penguin Group (USA) Inc., 375 Hudson Street, New York, New York 10014, USA
Penguin Group (Canada), 90 Eglinton Avenue East, Suite 700, Toronto, Ontario, Canada
M4P 2Y3 (a division of Pearson Penguin Canada Inc.)
Penguin Ireland, 25 St Stephen's Green, Dublin 2, Ireland
(a division of Penguin Books Ltd)
Penguin Group (Australia), 250 Camberwell Road, Camberwell, Victoria 3124,
Australia (a division of Pearson Australia Group Pty Ltd)
Penguin Books India Pvt Ltd, 11 Community Centre, Panchsheel Park,
New Delhi – 110 017, India
Penguin Group (NZ), 67 Apollo Drive, Rosedale, North Shore 0632, New Zealand
(a division of Pearson New Zealand Ltd)
Penguin Books (South Africa) (Pty) Ltd, 24 Sturdee Avenue, Rosebank,
Johannesburg 2196, South Africa

Penguin Books Ltd, Registered Offices: 80 Strand, London WC2R 0RL, England

www.penguin.com

First published 2008
1

The extract from 'In Oregon' in *A Space Filled with Moving*, (1992) by Maggie Anderson that appears on p. 51 is reproduced by kind permission of the University of Pittsburgh Press.

The extract from 'Niobe' in *Tales from Ovid* (1997) by Ted Hughes that appears on p. 66 is reproduced by kind permission of Faber and Faber Ltd/The Ted Hughes Estate.

Every effort has been made to trace copyright holders and to obtain their permission for the use of copyright material. The publisher apologizes for any errors or omissions and would be grateful to be notified of any corrections that should be incorporated in future editions of this book.

The moral right of the author has been asserted

Set in 11/13 pt PostScript Adobe Minion
Typeset by Rowland Phototypesetting Ltd, Bury St Edmunds, Suffolk
Printed in England by Clays Ltd, St Ives plc

ISBN: 978–0–141–02821–7

Preface

This book developed naturally from my work on *How to Write Better English* in this series of Writers' Guides, published in 2005. The earlier book dealt with the subject of good English on a thematic basis, starting with words and progressing through the grammatical hierarchy of phrases, clauses, sentences, and so on. Included in *Better English* was a hitlist of about thirty or so problems relating to particular words and phrases, and the present book picks up where that chapter left off. It is in fact a much bigger word-based hitlist in its own right, including items such as *agree to* and *with*, correct use of *barely*, *hardly*, and *scarcely*, the problem of *different from* and *to*, vogue words such as *iconic*, and so on, and dealing with various aspects of usage, spelling and inflection, confusable words (*complement* and *compliment*, *fortunate* and *fortuitous*), and so on. There are some thematic headings in the book (for example, it seemed better to group spelling problems in one place rather than scatter the individual words throughout the book), but overall the emphasis is on particular words and phrases that cause problems and give rise to error.

A major feature of both books is the use of real examples of English taken from actual usage in literature, journalism, and broadcasting. These afford a naturalness that cannot be achieved in examples made up by the compiler, which always seem stilted and artificial by comparison. I have also made extensive use of the British National Corpus, a database of some 100 million words of British English assembled by a consortium of publishers and academic institutions in the UK.

As in *Better English*, a glossary has been added explaining the main terms used in the text. This has enabled me to use the standard metalanguage of linguistic terminology without, I hope, leaving the reader confused. There is no way of describing the language adequately without using names such as *noun*, *verb*, *adjective*, and even *determiner*, and readers will quickly become familiar with them with the aid of this glossary. The book as a whole is intended to be self-sufficient, but readers will find some topics explored more fully in *Better English*, and in other books in the series. I have included cross-references to them in order to avoid repeating large amounts of material.

I would like to thank John English, who has copy-edited this book and helped to improve it as a result, and Ellie Smith, who has seen it through into production.

Robert Allen
Edinburgh, 2007

Note: The abbreviations AmE and BrE are used for American English and British English respectively.

a, an

Choice between *a* and *an* causes difficulty when the following word (typically a noun or adjective) begins with a vowel or an *h*. Here are some basic rules:

- If the word begins with a consonant, including *h* if this is pronounced, you use *a*: *a book, a happy time, a history lesson, a NATO exercise, a yacht.*
- If the word begins with a vowel, or an *h* that is not pronounced, you use *an*: *an apple, an echo, an honour, an issue, an overture, an urn.*
- If the word begins with a vowel that is pronounced with a *y* sound, you use *a*: *a European, a uniform, a UN resolution.*
- If the word begins with a consonant but is pronounced with an initial vowel sound, you use *an*. These are mainly abbreviations in which the first letter is pronounced as itself, and the letters involved are *f, l, m, n, r, s,* and *x* (all letters that have a vowel sound before them when you say them by themselves): *an FA ruling, an LP, an MEP, an NUJ conference, an RPO concert, an X-ray.*
- There is a special problem with words that begin with *h* when the stress is on a syllable other than the first, because then the *h* sound is less marked (compare the sounds in **history** and **historical**) and usage varies between *a* and *an*: *a historical fact* or *an historical fact, a horrendous mistake* or *an horrendous mistake.* The strong tendency now is to use *a* and not *an* (which is beginning to sound like affectation). In writing, the important point is to be consistent.

abbreviations

Abbreviations are used in all languages to express a word or name in a shorter form, either for convenience or to give it a special meaning or status. The main types of abbreviation in English are:

- initialisms (e.g. *TUC*, *GP*, *VDU*)
- acronyms (e.g. *Aids*, *radar*)
- shortenings (e.g. *Weds.*, *Prof.*, *bus*, *zoo*)
- contractions (e.g. *Mr*, *St*)

➤ *Initialisms* (e.g. *a.m.*, *TUC*, *MP*, *VDU*) are abbreviations made from the initial letters (or sometimes other letters) of the words they stand for. When spoken, they are usually pronounced as separate letters. Many of these are names of organizations (*TUC = Trades Union Congress*), and others are technical names that are too unwieldy for repeated use in their full form (*VDU = Visual Display Unit*, *DNA = deoxyribonucleic acid*). Abbreviations of the chief compass points (e.g. *NNW* = north-north-west) are also initialisms.

The practice of punctuating initialisms with full stops (as in *T.U.C.*, *G.P.*, *N.N.E.*) has largely disappeared, although it occurs in older printing. Full stops should be omitted when all the initials are capitals, and they can also be omitted in other cases that are familiar or established, for example names of academic degrees (*Ph D*, *M Sc*) and names of government departments (*DoH* = Department of Health).

To make a plural form of an initialism, you add an *-s* without an apostrophe (e.g. *GPs* rather than *GP's*).

Possessives are formed in the usual way (e.g. *GP's* singular, *GPs'* plural):

a conference of Scottish GPs
the GP's surgery (one GP)
the GPs' surgery (more than one GP)

➤ *Acronyms* (e.g. *Aids*, *derv*, *ISA*, *scuba*, *NATO*) are initialisms that have become words in their own right and are pronounced as ordinary words and not as a sequence of letters (e.g. **eye**-ser, **scoo**-ber, **nay**-toh). Many are technical terms or the names of institutions. They are often written with small letters, and can form plurals when appropriate. Some shortenings end up as a mixture of abbreviation and acronym, e.g. *CD-ROM* (pronounced see-dee-**rom**).

Some acronyms have humorous connotations, such as *nimby* (= not in my back yard, for a person who supports a cause as long as it does not affect them), *yuppie* (= young urban professional), and *tina* (= there is no alternative).

Below is a list of some common acronyms. Some are the names of institutions and others are general words:

Aids	acquired immune deficiency syndrome
Anzac	Australian and New Zealand Army Corps
ASH	Action on Smoking and Health
Bupa	British United Provident Association
ISA	individual savings account
laser	light amplification by stimulated emission of radiation
NATO	North Atlantic Treaty Organization
nimby	not in my back yard

Ofcom	Office of Communications (and other *Of-* bodies)
Opec	Organization of Petroleum Exporting Countries
quango	quasi (or quasi-autonomous) non-governmental organization
quasar	quasi-stellar (object)
radar	radio detection and ranging
SALT	Strategic Arms Limitations Talks
scuba	self-contained underwater breathing apparatus
tina	there is no alternative
UNESCO	United Nations Educational, Scientific, and Cultural Organization
WYSIWYG	what you see is what you get (in computing)
yuppie	young urban professional

Some abbreviations are treated as both initialisms and acronyms (e.g. *VAT* = value added tax, which can be pronounced as its three letters or as a single word 'vat').

➤ *Shortenings* are words that are cut at one end or at both ends. There are two kinds: those that are still in effect abbreviations (such as *Thurs.* and *Prof.*), and those that form words in their own right (sometimes called 'clippings', such as *fridge* and *zoo*).

Abbreviation shortenings
These still count as abbreviations rather than as words. Examples are days of the week (*Weds.* = Wednesday) and months of the year (*Oct.* = October), single-letter abbreviations such as *p.* (= page) and *l.* (= line) followed by a number reference, and technical abbreviations such as *dim.* (= diminuendo) in music. These

are normally spelt with a full point. Some single-letter abbreviations double the letter to form a plural, e.g. *pp.* (= pages).

Initials in names can be spelt with or without full stops (*M. J. Tate* or *M J Tate*), but in handwriting a full stop helps to make the name clearer.

Words that are shortened as titles before names, such as *Prof.* (= Professor) and *Capt.* (= Captain) are also spelt with a full stop (as in *Prof. M. Smith* and *Col. R. P. Digby*), unlike contracted titles such as *Dr* and *Mr* (see next section).

Word shortenings
Some shortenings have become words in their own right, often superseding the fuller form in ordinary usage. In some cases (e.g. *blog, bus, cello, fridge, gym, vet,* and *zoo*) they have become the normal word to use, while the full forms on which they are based (*weblog, omnibus, violoncello, refrigerator, gymnasium, veterinary surgeon,* and *zoological gardens*) are generally reserved for formal contexts, such as names and titles. The use of apostrophes in shortened forms (as in *'cello* and *'flu*) has largely disappeared, although it may be found in older printing. (The nautical word *fo'c's'le* = 'forecastle' is an exception, because it looks odd without apostrophes; but *bo'sun* = 'boatswain' tends now to be written as *bosun*.)

Other shortenings have special meanings or connotations not shared by the full form (e.g. a *quad* is a quadrangle in a college, and *spec* is used in the idiom *on spec*). On the other hand, some shortenings (such as *info*, *ref*, and *telly*) still seem casual and should only be used in informal contexts.

Below is a fuller list of shortened words. (You will see that some shortenings have ousted the original words completely; we always refer now to a *cab* or a *taxi* and never to a *cabriolet* or *taximeter cab*.)

ad	advertisement
bike	bicycle
bookie	bookmaker
bra	brassière
bus	omnibus
cab	cabriolet
cello	violoncello
cinema	cinematograph
cox	coxswain
curio	curiosity
deli	delicatessen
exam	examination
flu	influenza
fridge	refrigerator
gym	gymnasium
hippo	hippopotamus
info	information
kilo	kilogram
lib	(women's etc.) liberation
mike	microphone
perm	permanent wave
phone	telephone
photo	photograph
polio	poliomyelitis
pram	perambulator

prefab	prefabricated building
prep	preparation
pub	public house
quad	quadrangle
ref	referee
rep	representative
rhino	rhinoceros
spec	speculation
specs	spectacles
taxi	taximeter cab
telly	television
vet	veterinary surgeon
viva	viva voce (exam)

➤ In **contractions**, letters from the middle of the word are omitted. A common form of contraction is in titles put before names, e.g. *Dr* (= doctor), *Mr* (= Mister), and *St* (= saint). The abbreviation *no.* (= number) is a contraction of the Latin word *numero* (a form of the word *numerus*). It is now less common to mark contractions with full points (as in *Dr*), except to avoid confusion with other words (as with *no.*). These contractions are simply conventions used without involving any particular level of formality or informality.

Another kind of contraction involves merging two words with an apostrophe marking the missing letters, e.g. *didn't* (= did not), *they've* (= they have), and *wouldn't* (= would not). These contractions reflect the practice of informal conversation and are perfectly acceptable in everyday writing, such as a note or a personal letter, or in recording conversation. In more formal writing, such as a job application or a business letter, it is advisable to avoid them as they suggest a familiarity with the person addressed and this is not usually appropriate:

? *I've enclosed a list of referees and I'd be glad if you'd let me know before you contact them.*

✓ *I have enclosed a list of referees and I would be glad if you would let me know before you contact them.*

Longer contractions, such as *should've* (= should have) and double contractions such as *mayn't've* (= may not have) sometimes occur in print (especially in fiction) but they are awkward and should be avoided.

➢ **Abbreviations for weights and measures** and **abbreviations used in science** are usually written without full stops, e.g. *cm* (= centimetre or centimetres), *lb* (= pound or pounds weight), *kg* (= kilogram or kilograms), *MHz* (= megahertz), *mph* (= miles per hour). But some non-metric units are written with a full stop when leaving it out might be confusing, e.g. *in.* (= inch or inches), *mi.* (= mile or miles).

Metric units have plural forms that are identical to the singular, e.g. *1 cm* and *50 cm*, but in. (= inch) and *yd* (= yard) can have plural forms *ins* (= inches) and *yds* (= yards). The form *ft* (= foot) is strictly speaking a contraction, and the plural form is also *ft* (= feet).

Chemical symbols are always spelt with an initial capital letter and without a full stop, e.g. *Ca* (= calcium) and *Li* (= lithium).

ability, capability, capacity

These words overlap in meaning and dictionaries tend to define one in terms of the others. *Ability* is the most common word, occurring typically twice as often as *capacity* and three times as often as *capability*. *Ability* is more appropriate as a human attribute whereas *capacity* has a more logistical ring and also conveys a notion of size:

*Regardless of **ability**, all yogis gain the same benefits from their efforts.*
*Many respondents are unprepared for the impact of their injuries on their long-term **capacity** for work.*

Ability and *capacity* go more naturally with a *to*-infinitive than does *capability*, which (in BrE) is more usually followed by *of* with an *-ing* verb:

*Christians, it seems, have an incredible **ability** to invent rules and regulations.*
*Not everyone has the **capacity** to write a good tune.*
*We removed a declared enemy of America, who had the **capability** of producing weapons of mass destruction.*

Capacity can also be used with *for* and an *-ing* verb:

*The human **capacity** for destroying the planet.*

-able, -ible

These are typical endings of adjectives that mean 'able to be –' or 'fit to be –' or something similar: for example, *adaptable* means 'able to be adapted', *deplorable* means 'fit to be deplored', and *digestible* means 'able to be digested'. These suffixes are typically added to verbs (*adapt, deplore, digest*) and are based on Latin endings *-abilis* and *-ibilis*.

The suffix *-able* is known as an active suffix because new words continue to be formed with it, and you can make up words to suit your purpose with it: for example, *knowledgeable* (exceptionally formed from a noun, *knowledge*, and not a verb; others are *marriage-able* and *peaceable*) was first used in the 1820s. In more recent times *programmable* came into use in connection with data processing in the 1950s, and the technology of the early 1980s gave rise to the need for *microwaveable* and *photocopiable* (both of which caused a spelling uncertainty for a while).

Here is a list of the most common adjectives ending in *-able*:

abominable	ascribable
actionable	assessable
adaptable	atonable
administrable	available
admittable (*also* admissible)	bearable
adorable	believable
advisable	blameable
agreeable	bribable
alienable	bridgeable
amenable	calculable
amiable	capable
analysable	changeable
appreciable	chargeable
arguable	clubbable

collectable
comfortable
conceivable
conferrable
confinable
consolable
contractable (*of a disease; see also* contractible)
copiable
creatable
curable
datable
debatable
declinable
defendable (*in literal meanings; see also* defensible)
deferable
definable
delineable
demonstrable
demurrable
deniable
dependable
desirable
despicable
developable
dilatable
dispensable
disposable
dissolvable
drivable

durable
dutiable
eatable
educable (= *able to be educated; see also* educible)
endorsable
equable
evadable
excisable
excitable
excusable
expandable (*also* expansible)
expendable
expiable
extendable (*also* extendible, extensible)
finable
flammable
foreseeable
forgettable
forgivable
framable
gettable
giveable
hireable
illimitable
immovable
immutable
impalpable
impassable (= *unable to be crossed; see also* impassible)
impeccable

imperturbable
implacable
impressionable
improvable
indefatigable
indescribable
indispensable
indubitable
inflammable
inflatable
inimitable
insufferable
irreconcilable
irreplaceable
justifiable
knowledgeable
laughable
leviable
likeable
liveable
losable
lovable
machinable
malleable
manageable
manoeuvrable
marriageable
measurable
mistakable
movable
mutable
nameable

noticeable
objectionable
obtainable
operable
palatable
payable
peaceable
penetrable
perishable
permeable
persuadable (*also* persuasible)
pleasurable
preferable
prescribable
preventable
pronounceable
provable
rateable
readable
receivable
reconcilable
rectifiable
registrable
regrettable
reliable
removable
reputable
retractable
saleable
scalable
serviceable
sizeable

solvable
statutable
storable
suitable
superannuable
timeable
tolerable
traceable
tradable
transferable
tuneable

unconscionable
undeniable
unexceptionable
unget-at-able
unknowable
unmistakable
unscalable
unshakeable
unthinkable
usable

HISTORICAL NOTE – Some words ending in *-able* do not quite follow the normal grammatical pattern: for example, *laughable* means 'fit to be laughed *at*' and *reliable* means 'able to be relied *on*'. In the nineteenth century some grammarians regarded these forms as improper, because they failed to take account of the *at* and the *on*: you laugh *at* something and rely *on* someone. But *reliable* and *laughable*, and others such as *dependable* and *unthinkable*, have become a fixed part of the language and few people are aware of this distinction today.

Some adjectives having these types of meaning are formed with *-ible* instead of *-able*. There are far fewer of these and generally speaking no new ones are being formed. In many cases the whole word is taken from a Latin word ending in *-ibilis*, so the word came ready-formed into English. For example, our word *horrible* is based on a Latin word *horribilis*.

Here is a list of the most common adjectives ending in *-ible*:

accessible

admissible (*also* admittable)

apprehensible

audible

collapsible

compatible

comprehensible

contemptible

contractible (= *able to be shrunk; see also* contractable)

convertible

credible

deductible

defensible (*of an argument or opinion; see also* defendable)

destructible

dirigible

edible

educible (= *able to be educed; see also* educable)

eligible

fallible

feasible

flexible

forcible (*better than* forceable)

fusible

gullible

horrible

illegible

impassible (*unfeeling; see also* impassable)

imperceptible

implausible

impossible

inaccessible

inadmissible

inaudible

incompatible

incomprehensible

incontrovertible

incorrigible

incorruptible

incredible

indefensible

indelible

indestructible

indivisible

inedible

ineligible

inexhaustible

inexpressible

infallible

inflexible

insensible

intangible

intelligible

invincible

invisible

irascible

irreducible

irrepressible

irresistible

irresponsible

legible

miscible

negligible

ostensible

perceptible

permissible

persuasible (*also* persuadable)

plausible

possible

reprehensible

responsible

risible

sensible

submersible

suggestible

susceptible

tangible

terrible

unintelligible

vincible

visible

USAGE NOTE – Notice that nearly all the negative forms (i.e. words meaning 'not – ') begin with *in-* or *im-* or *ir-* and not *un-*: for example, *inedible, implausible, irreducible*.

Words that end in *e* (such as *arrange* and *blame*) sometimes lose and sometimes keep this *e* when you add *-able*. Words ending in *-ce* or *-dge* usually keep the final *e* to preserve the soft sound: *bridgeable, changeable, knowledgeable, manageable, noticeable, serviceable*. But *datable, lovable, movable*, and others lose the final *e* because the sound is clear enough without it.

Here is a list of adjectives that normally keep the *e*:

acknowledgeable

arrangeable

blameable

bridgeable

challengeable

changeable

chargeable

danceable

dyeable

effaceable

embraceable

enforceable

exchangeable

forgeable

gaugeable

handleable

ineffaceable

irreplaceable

knowledgeable

likeable

liveable

manageable

marriageable

microwaveable

mineable

mortgageable

nameable

noticeable

peaceable

pronounceable

rateable

rechargeable

renounceable

replaceable

rideable

saleable

salvageable

serviceable

shapeable

sizeable

sliceable

smokeable

spongeable

stageable

stateable

tameable

traceable

tuneable

unchallengeable

unchangeable

unlikeable

unmanageable

unpronounceable

unshakeable

untraceable

wipeable

And now the most common words that lose the *e*:

datable	movable
drivable	reconcilable
finable	savable
hatable	takable
immovable	tradable
irreconcilable	unlovable
lovable	unmistakable
makable	usable
mistakable	

When a word ends in a single consonant (chiefly b, d, f, g, l, m, n, p, r, s, and t) you double the consonant when it follows a single-letter vowel with the stress on it: e.g. *programmable, forgettable*.

For more details of words of these types, see George Davidson's *Improve Your Spelling* in this series of *Writers' Guides*.

abstract nouns

These are nouns that stand for an idea or state or process, such as *freedom*, *joy*, and *restitution*. Many adjectives can be turned into abstract nouns by adding -*ness*, e.g. *happiness*, *tenderness*, or an instance of something: *kindness* is the state of being kind and *a kindness* is a kind action. Other abstract nouns are formed with suffixes auch as -*tion* (*abolition*, *derivation*, *restitution*) and these can also denote an instance of an action as well as a state or idea.

Abstract nouns are useful in condensing a notion into a single word, but they can become excessive and this tends to produce dull and off-putting sentences such as the following:

Decentralization will mean innovation and experimentation.

This as a challenging or stimulating statement is dead in the water. How much better to unpack these abstract nouns and bring the real meaning to the surface:

If we decentralize our activities we can be more innovative and have more scope for trying out new methods.

This is longer but a great deal more effective. If space is a problem, however, there is a halfway house:

If we decentralize we can be more innovative and experiment.

abuse, misuse

Both words are used as noun and verb:

*Demand in our NHS will remain insatiable until there is a change for the better in the attitude of those who **abuse** [verb] the system.*
*It is a crushing analysis of a decade of deception, dishonesty and **abuse** [noun] of power.*
*Such a vast database is sure to **be misused** [verb].*
*This, I feel, is a flagrant **misuse** [noun] of public funds.*

Their meanings overlap considerably, but it is useful to bear in mind a general distinction that *abuse* tends to imply use for a wrong purpose or to serve a wrong end, whereas *misuse* implies a wrong type of use. *Abuse* (especially as a noun) has stronger connotations of offence against people (as in *verbal abuse*) and institutions (as in the first example above), and has developed sinister meanings in recent years in two particular contexts, the sexual mistreatment of children and drug addiction (as in *substance abuse*). This should be borne in mind in making a choice between the two words.

accept, except

To *accept* something is to take it or agree to it (*conditions we could never accept*; *the generally accepted view*); to *except* something is to make an exception of it (*no great painters if you except Goya*). *Except* is more common as a preposition (with or without *for*: *all the painters except Goya* or *except for Goya*) or in the form *excepting* (*each month excepting February*). Alternatives to *except* (as a preposition), *except for*, and *excepting* are *excluding*, *apart from*, and *other than*.

according as *or* to

According to is much more common; it can mean either 'on the authority of' (as in the first example below) or 'in accordance with' or 'in proportion to' (as in the second).

*The UK's reserves of peat bogs are much less than previously thought, **according to** a new survey.*
*People react **according to** their temperaments.*

According to is known as a complex preposition, because it has the role of prepositions such as *by* or *with*. The combination *according as*, which is much less common, is a conjunction and is followed by a clause containing a verb:

*The result is a stroke or a heart attack **according as** the event is in the blood system of the brain or the heart muscle.*

Although this construction used to be frowned on, it has become well established and can no longer be faulted. However, it is best to avoid the extended construction *according as to*, which you sometimes find in more technical writing, and use *depending on* instead:

? *Beliefs are acceptable or not **according as to** [✓ depending on] whether they succeed in their goal of conforming to reality.*

acknowledge, acknowledgement

These are spelt with -*ck*-, and the noun is spelt with three *e*'s (although *acknowledgment* is a permitted variant).

active *and* passive

When the subject of the verb performs the action, as in *Julia has sent an email*, the verb is said to be in the active voice. In the passive voice, the object of the action becomes the grammatical subject, and the performer of the action, if stated at all, is introduced by a preposition, normally *by*, as in *The email has been sent by Julia*. We could simply say *The email has been sent*, without specifying the sender: one reason that the passive is sometimes preferred!

USAGE NOTE – Passive verbs are formed with the verb *be*, and other verbs are used to form so-called 'semi-passives' in which the past participle of the verb (typically ending in *-ed* or *-t*) is like an adjective (e.g. *He got burnt* and *They seem amused*).

Passive verbs can be effective when it is the recipient of an action rather than the performer that is the main point of what you want to say. In the example given above, the main point is that an email was sent, and it might not matter much who sent it. But some uses of the passive have a stilted and awkward effect on writing, and can be tainted by associations of vagueness and obfuscation to be found in official documents and reports (e.g. *It is recommended that you take the action described*).

Avoid passives with verbs such as *attempt*, *begin*, *desire*, *endeavour*, *propose*, *threaten*, and others that involve constructions with a *to*-infinitive:

? *Their plan was begun to be implemented.*

A fully active construction should be used instead:

✓ *They began to implement their plan.*

Other verbs, such as *expect*, *intend*, and *order*, which are grammatically more versatile, will allow a double passive construction. For example, we can say:

✓ *They ordered the offenders to be punished.*

and therefore a double passive form is allowed:

✓ *The offenders were ordered to be punished.*

actual, actually

These can be useful words that reinforce a point, especially to distinguish something real from something hypothetical or notional:

*The **actual** cost proved much higher than the estimates.*
*Expectations could never live up to the **actual** event.*

But *actual*, and even more the adverb *actually*, tends to be overused as a kind of sentence filler without any real meaning. This is more acceptable in speech, where it can help with the rhythm of the sentence, but you should avoid it in writing:

? *Special care is needed before and after the patient's **actual** discharge from hospital.*
? *The plan may **actually** backfire.*
? *What time will they **actually** arrive?*

(Take out *actual* or *actually* and you have saved a word in each sentence with no loss of meaning.)

However, *actually* has a useful role in contrastive contexts that distinguish reality from an idea or expectation:

✓ *It looks improvised but it **actually** [= in reality, as it happened] took a great deal of care to make it.*

Dr Firmin's manners were so good, his forehead was so high, his frill so fresh, his hands so white and slim, that

for some considerable time we ingenuously admired
him; and it was not without a pang that we came to
view him as he actually was – no, not as he actually
was – no man whose early nurture was kindly can
judge quite impartially the man who has been kind to
him in boyhood.

William Thackeray, *The Adventures of Philip*, 1862

acute, chronic

An *acute* illness or difficulty is one that comes rapidly
to a crisis, whereas a *chronic* one persists for a long
time. This distinction is important and the two words
are not at all interchangeable.

-acy, -asy

Much the more common of these two noun endings
is *-acy*, which occurs in *fallacy*, *intimacy*, *legacy*, *literacy*,
piracy, *privacy*, and all the words in *-cracy* (meaning
'power') such as *bureaucracy* and *democracy*.

Four words end in *-asy*: *apostasy* ('the abandonment
of a belief'), *ecstasy*, *fantasy*, and *idiosyncrasy*. In all
these cases the ending is not a distinct suffix but is
based on Latin or Greek nouns ending in *-asia* or *-asis*.
Ecstasy is made up of words meaning 'standing outside
oneself'. *Idiosyncrasy* (which comes from the Greek
words *idios* 'one's own' and *krasis* 'mixture') is especially important to note as it is tempting to spell it
-cracy on the false analogy of the *-cracy* 'power' words
mentioned above.

AD, BC, BCE, CE

The abbreviations BC and AD traditionally added to
dates before and after the birth of Christ are gradually
giving way to the culturally more neutral alternatives BCE ('before common era') and CE ('[of the]
common era'). For some these smack of political cor-
rectness, but they have the advantage that both can be
put after the number representing the date, whereas
with AD there has always been the problem of whether
to put it after the date, like BC, e.g. 1066 AD, or
(strictly more correctly, because it is short for Latin
anno Domini 'in the year of the Lord') before it, e.g.
AD 1066. It had become general usage to write 'the
second century AD', but it is simpler and less open to
the objections of purists to put 'the second century
CE' (or in full, 'of the common era').

adherence, adhesion

*Creationism enjoys scant **adherence** in Britain. But how about
ghosts?*
*In parts of the city, new surfaces have been laid to reduce the
adhesion of chewing gum.*

Both words come from the Latin verb *haerere* 'to stick'
(with the added prefix *ad-*) which is also the source of
our verb *adhere*. *Adherence* is mostly used in meanings
to do with beliefs, loyalties, laws and rules, etc., whereas
adhesion implies physical contact such as the sticking
or gluing together of two surfaces, the grip of wheels
on the road, and so on. The distinction is not clear-cut,

however, and *adhesion* also has its figurative uses, although the notion of physical sticking is always nearer the surface than it is with *adherence*:

*There is a growing belief that caring for the environment is becoming a new form of community **adhesion**, binding people together in a common purpose.*

adjacent, adjoining, contiguous

All three words have the general meaning 'next to' in position, but there are important differences. A building or room is *adjacent* to another when it is nearby but not necessarily joined to it, an *adjacent room* can be across a corridor, and *adjacent tables* are next to each other with a space between. The word needed if there is physical contact is *adjoining*, and as a verb participle it can also govern a following noun rather like a preposition:

*She had a room **adjoining** his, and there was even a connecting door.*

Adjacent needs the help of the preposition *to*, and the effect is less intimate:

*The marine side of the port **adjacent to** the new quays will need to be dredged to 10 m to provide access for deeper draught ships.*

admission, admittance

The meanings of these words overlap, but *admission* has one major advantage over *admittance*: it is 'countable', which means we can talk about *an admission* and *admissions* (plural) as well as plain *admission*, where with *admittance* all there is is *admittance* (usually with *no* before it). *Admission* is also the only one used attributively (i.e. before another noun, as in *admission charge, policy, process, ticket*, etc.). As regards meaning and context, *admission* is typically used positively of access to public places or institutions (either physical places or the services or rights they exercise), whereas *admittance* conveys notions of privacy:

While reform of its care homes was made a requirement of Romania's **admission** *to the EU, no such demand was issued to Bulgaria.*

Crime statistics, house prices, school results, insurance claims and even hospital **admissions** *are fed into the equation.*

A guest list has been drawn up and identities will be checked. There will be no **admittance** *on the door on the day.*

In the meaning 'acknowledgement or acceptance as true' (corresponding to the verb *admit*), *admission* is the word to use, not *admittance*:

✓ *The statement was a clear* **admission** *that salmon farms are a threat to wild fish.*

✗ *By her own* **admittance** [✓ *on her own admission*], *she's not blessed with the best of complexions.*

adopted, adoptive

Adopted refers to the child legally taken in by new parents, and *adoptive* to the parents who do the adopting.

adverbs
position of adverbs

The term 'adverb' covers a wide range of words that modify the meaning of adjectives, verbs, other adverbs, and whole sentences. Many adverbs end in *-ly* and mean 'in a – way or manner' (e.g. *happily* = in a happy manner, *honestly* = in an honest way, *slowly* = in a slow manner, *tacitly* = in a tacit way, etc.). These cause little trouble, typically coming after the verb or before the adjective they qualify:

He went happily off to bed.
They behaved honestly all their lives.
She cycled slowly up the road.
We felt seriously alarmed.

Problems arise with so-called 'adverbs of degree or respect', such as *usually*, *often*, *rarely*, and – in particular – *only*. The natural position of this kind of adverb, when it qualifies a whole statement, is before the verb:

I usually go to the shops on Saturday.
They often seem to be late.
I only wanted to say hello.

Sometimes, however, the logical position is not the same as the natural position, and some language purists insist that the logical position should take precedence:

[natural position] *We only have time for a quick chat.*
[logical position] *We have time only for a quick chat.*

It is called the logical position because *only* logically

applies to the quick chat rather than to having time. In some sentences, it is argued, there is the possibility of misunderstanding:

We only visit the park in fine weather.

This can mean 'we visit the park but only in fine weather [and we may do other things then as well]' or 'when the weather is fine all we do is visit the park [and we may visit the park at other times as well]', or even notionally 'we only *visit* the park in fine weather [i.e. we don't play games in it]'. Depending on the sense, this should be reordered as

We visit the park only in fine weather.
In fine weather we only visit the park.

The third meaning, which is the least likely, would be expressed as

All we do in the park in fine weather is visit it.

You only need to do this rearranging if the sense is otherwise unclear, because *only* (as used earlier in this very sentence) typically refers forward to the continuation of the sentence (here, *only* refers to 'if the sense is otherwise unclear' and not to 'need to do this').

This rare species is only found on the western seaboard.

This order is satisfactory because it is clear that *only* here refers ahead to 'on the western seaboard' and not specifically to the verb 'found', although for more emphasis you can say:

This rare species is found only on the western seaboard.

Or, even more emphatically:

It is only on the western seaboard that this rare species is found.

sentence adverbs

Some adverbs, including *clearly*, *sadly*, *honestly*, *frankly*, *hopefully*, and *thankfully*, can be used to qualify a whole sentence and not just a word or phrase in the sentence. In this role the adverb is typically put in initial or final position (or close to these) and stands grammatically outside the main structure, reflecting the opinion of the speaker rather than modifying anything in the sentence:

***Clearly**, these are all developing countries.*
***Sadly**, that is not possible.*
*He **honestly** wouldn't hurt a fly.*
*I don't know why they did it, **frankly**.*

The two that cause the most trouble are *thankfully* and, in particular, *hopefully*:

***Thankfully**, no damage was done to the building.*
*He was not in control of his life, but that was **hopefully** going to change.*

The reason may be that neither of these can be resolved into a phrase such as 'in a – way' or 'as is –' in the way that the others can to a greater or lesser degree. The first sentence above, for example, can be resolved into 'As is clear, these are developing countries'; but *hopefully* and *thankfully* can only be resolved into the passive constructions 'as is to be hoped' and 'as is to

be thanked' and even these expansions are somewhat
forced. But there is no reason why every adverb (a
catch-all grammatical term if ever there was one)
should have to be resolved in this way.

In the case of *hopefully*, the argument is sometimes
adduced that the meaning can be ambiguous, because
hopefully also means 'in a hopeful way'. While mild
ambiguity is possible (e.g. *They are hopefully awaiting
good news*), this is rare and can in particular cases be
resolved by rephrasing (e.g. either *We hope they are
awaiting good news* or *They are hopeful of good news*).
This should not be a reason for dismissing its role as
a sentence adverb altogether. But since this usage is
controversial, it is best avoided when communicating
more formally with people whose language preferences
you do not know.

adverse, averse

Adverse means 'harmful' or 'unfavourable': *adverse
weather conditions, an adverse effect.*
Averse means 'strongly opposed' and is followed by *to*:
they are not averse to taking risks.

advice, advise

The noun is *advice*: *the only advice I can offer*. The verb
is *advise*: *She advised me to seek help.*

aeroplane / airplane

Aeroplane (ae-) is BrE; *airplane* is chiefly AmE.

affect, effect

These words are commonly confused. It is simplest to start with *effect*, which is a noun and verb; as a noun it means 'something caused, a result or consequence' (as in *Their education had little effect on them*; also *in effect* and *to take effect*). There are also particular meanings, for example *special effects* (in drama, the cinema, etc.). The verb *effect* means 'to cause or bring about' (as in *to effect change*). We can then explain *affect* as a verb (predominantly) meaning 'to have an effect on' (as in *The news affected them badly* and *These new findings affect our conclusions*); again there are special uses, e.g. *to affect an illness* is to pretend to be ill. *Affect* is also a noun in the special context of psychology, where it means 'the conscious subjective aspect of an emotion considered as influencing behaviour'; but for most of the time it works to think of *affect* as primarily a verb that can also be used as a noun and *effect* as primarily a noun that can also be used as a verb.

afflict, inflict

Both words mean 'to bring unpleasant or unwanted circumstances', but they have different constructions. *Afflict* has the victim of the unpleasantness as its grammatical object, whereas *inflict* refers to the unpleasantness itself, with the victim optionally expressed by means of *on* (or occasionally *upon*):

*The short-tailed shrew can **inflict** an unpleasant bite with the help of spittle from its venomous salivary glands.*

*I think he is wrong to **inflict** his belief on everybody else.*
*Nerves **afflict** most people in some way.*

Afflict is common in the passive, in the form *be afflicted with* or *by*:

*Neither of her brothers **is afflicted** in any way **by** claustro-phobia.*
*Pound **was afflicted with** remorse and guilt at the shape his life had taken.*

aftermath

The proper meaning of this curious word is 'the period after a major event or disaster', which has little to do with its original meaning of 'a second growth of forage after the harvest of an earlier crop'. You will have a hard job finding examples of the word used in this way; it has been given over entirely to the figurative meaning. This, in contrast to the original optimistic meaning, tends to relate to the sequels to events that are unpleasant or threatening:

*The **aftermath** of a fire is always sad.*
*Beyond 1945 and its immediate **aftermath** was the outline of a future permeated with hope.*

ageing

Excessive alcohol hastens the ageing process.

This is the better spelling because it preserves the root word *age* more effectively, although *aging* is more common, especially in AmE.

aggravate

This means properly 'to make a (bad) situation worse':

*Import restrictions would simply **aggravate** the problem.*

This meaning has been largely superseded by a secondary meaning which transfers the action of the verb from the situation to the person affected, as a synonym of 'annoy' or 'irritate'. A verbal adjective *aggravating* has also arisen in the corresponding sense 'annoying':

*All these questions simply **aggravated** her.*
*How **aggravating** it was, being ignored like that.*

This usage is well established, but it is best to avoid it when writing more formally or for readers who are likely to take a strict view of matters of usage.

agnostic, atheist

An *atheist* is a person who denies the existence of God, or any guiding principle as creator of the universe, whereas *agnostics* declare that there is no way of knowing one way or the other. *Agnostic* has also developed a secondary meaning in other contexts, of a person who is impartial or open-minded about controversial matters:

The marketing agnostic on the task will often tease out unsuspected flaws in the campaign.

agree with *or* to

The verb *agree* can be followed by *to* or *with*, and it is important to remember the difference. To *agree with* someone is to have the same opinion as them; to *agree with* something is to share it as an opinion, and to *agree to* something is to approve of it or authorize it.

*I heartily **agree with** the writer of the article.*
*People don't have to **agree with** everything she says.*

*No one was willing to **agree to** a change of date.*

You cannot *agree to* someone, but you can *agree to* (i.e. consent to or approve of) someone (or someone's) *doing* something:

*We will **agree to** your joining the team on certain conditions.*

The verb *agree* can also take a *that*-clause (corresponding to *agree with*) and a *to*-infinitive (corresponding to *consent to*):

*Does the Prime Minister **agree that** we do not want the militarization of space?*
*He **agreed to** make a speech on stage after the performance.*

To *agree on* something (e.g. terms or a date) and to *agree* something both mean to reach agreement about it:

*Generally we **agree** on how the situation in Africa looks today.*
*The Community has **agreed** a programme of food credits.*

ahead of

This prepositional phrase is well established in the physical sense 'in front of' and in the figurative sense 'better than, superior to (in quality, performance, etc.)'. From the early part of the twentieth century come the meaning in relation to time (*ten minutes ahead of them*) and the phrase *ahead of one's* (or *its*) *time*, which may have been coined by George Bernard Shaw and has since become a cliché.

In a further – much more recent – development, *ahead of* has come to mean 'before' with the strongly anticipatory notion 'in preparation for' or 'taking account of':

*Interest is focused more closely on political uncertainty at home **ahead of** tonight's Europe vote.*
*Water utilities began mixed **ahead of** final figures due for some companies this week.*

This use, which originated in AmE, has a resoundingly journalistic ring and is not likely to find favour in general usage.

aim

In the sense 'try to achieve', followed by a verb, *aim* can be used with *at* and an *-ing* verb or by a *to*-infinitive:

*The forum **aims at** helping people to translate their ideas into positive action.*
*The mail-order company **is aiming to** fill a gap in the market with a range of swimwear in different styles.*

The *at* construction tends to conjure up a stronger image, and some language purists prefer it as being closer to the usage in physical senses to do with shooting at targets. The construction with *to* is based on the analogy of more abstract verbs such as *intend* and *seek* (and note that these can often be used instead, sometimes to better effect).

ain't

This negative form of the verb *be*, used to mean *am not*, *is not*, and *are not*, is widely regarded as a sure sign of illiteracy, and should be absolutely avoided. Exceptions apply when quoting, reproducing dialogue, and similar cases.

albeit

This useful word is often eschewed as a supposed archaism, but it conveniently combines the meanings contained in *if*, *though*, and *admittedly*. It has a useful role to play as an economical link word with more force than is provided by *if*, *while*, and other alternatives:

*The vaccine can cause brain damage, **albeit** in a tiny minority of children.*
*He managed to finish seventh, **albeit** three laps behind.*

Albeit that (followed by a clause) is found in legal and other official contexts; *even though* is a better choice in ordinary writing:

The Court did not deal with the remaining grounds of appeal, **albeit that** *submissions on all grounds of appeal had been made.*

alibi, alias

An *alibi* is properly 'the plea of having been somewhere else when a crime was committed', or the evidence of this plea:

Maria has an **alibi** *for the night Peter disappeared.*

Avoid using *alibi* loosely to mean 'plausible reason'; *excuse* is the better word to use in these cases:

✗ *These raids provided the* **alibi** [✓ *excuse*] *for declaring war.*
✗ *So far delivery has not lived up to expectations, and the* **alibis** [✓ *excuses*] *are running out.*

An *alias* is an assumed name by which a person, typically in public life, wants to be known in some connection:

The **alias** *he preferred was William P. Goode.*

Alias is also used adverbially before an assumed name in the sense 'also known as':

Eric Blair, **alias** *George Orwell.*

Note that *alias* should come before the assumed name and not before the actual name:

✗ *Jean Harlow,* **alias** *the teenager Harleen Carpenter from Kansas City.*

allegedly

Allegedly is a disclaiming word that has implications for the sentence formed around it. It is typically used in newspaper reports with reference to legal matters that are still undecided: *the accused man allegedly hit his victim with a baseball bat.* It is a comment word that applies to the whole surrounding content, so beware of producing incongruity as in the following:

? *An Iraqi prisoner has described how he was **allegedly** subjected to vicious beatings by British soldiers.*

One cannot describe something that only allegedly took place: the qualification needs to be put in the context of the prisoner's statement and not of the statement as a whole:

✓ *An Iraqi prisoner has described how, as he claims, he was subjected to vicious beatings by British soldiers.*

or

✓ *An Iraqi prisoner has described vicious beatings he claims he was subjected to by [or he received from] British soldiers.*

all right, alright

*Are you sure you are **all right**?*
*Is it **all right** to travel while pregnant?*
*I'm worried **all right**.*

All right (two words) is the better spelling, although *alright* (on the analogy of *almighty* and *altogether* – see next entry) is common, especially when the two words lose their full force, e.g. when used as a tag at the end of questions or to introduce a concession:

*She's just my friend, **alright**?*
***Alright**, I'll see you tomorrow.*

all together, altogether

There is an important difference in meaning between these two spellings.

Altogether is an adverb meaning 'in every way, entirely':

*You'll be making an **altogether** different type of journey.*
*Avoid that situation **altogether**.*

All together means 'everyone or everything together' and the two words keep their separate identity:

*I just needed to fit it **all together**.*

Notice the different spellings affect the meanings in the following sentences:

*There were ten desks **altogether**.* (There were ten in total.)
*There were ten desks **all together**.* (The desks were placed beside one another.)

allude, refer

These words overlap in meaning, but essentially to *allude to* something is to recall it casually or indirectly whereas to *refer to* it is to mention it explicitly.

Allude is typically used when a person or thing is

mentioned in some connection without being identified:

*One document still defies interpreters. I **allude** of course to the*
mysterious figure on a coin now in the British Museum.
At the end of the sixth book of the Faerie Queene, *Spenser*
***alludes** to some of the troubles his earlier work has caused*
through slanders.
*She has often darkly **alluded** to some form of abuse in her own*
formative years.

Refer, which is always the safer choice, is used when a
person or thing is being specifically named or identified
in some way:

*Many people **refer** to their vacuum cleaner as 'the Hoover'.*
*She says she likes to do it two or three times a month. I **refer***
to opera-going.
*In his Diaries, he **refers** to 'isotopes, whatever they might be'.*
A strange appointment as Secretary of State for Science in the
atomic age.

Meanwhile don't get distracted by the near-
homophone *elude*. This means more or less the
same as *escape* in the sense 'to fail to reach the memory
or understanding of (someone)', and the subject of
elude is usually something desired or aimed at:

*Heading a homicide inquiry is a prize which has always **eluded***
her.
*One issue that **eludes** control is knowing exactly what takes*
place behind the interviewing door.
*His name completely **eludes** me at the moment.*
*Certainty **eluded** them, and it eludes us still.*

allusion, reference, illusion, delusion

There is great scope for confusion in the use of these four words.

An *allusion* is an indirect reference to a person, thing, or idea, whereas a *reference* typically names or identifies it specifically:

*The committee made no **allusion** to the former President in its final conclusions.*

*He had a nice literary touch and wasn't averse to a Shakespearean **allusion**.*

*It comes as no surprise to find a tabloid newspaper defining women by **reference** to their sexual behaviour.*

*The Foreign Secretary said with **reference** to the dispute that the military option is not being excluded.*

An *illusion* is a false impression or notion, whether something seen or heard, or something thought. A *delusion* is a false belief or impression, a thought with which one deceives oneself.

*Reality itself is an **illusion** that our nervous system puts together for us.*

*It was almost warm enough to create the **illusion** of summer.*

*The catchphrase 'equality of opportunity' is a **delusion** concealing the injustice of our social hierarchy.*

*He did not want them to follow him under any false **delusion**.*

> Tom sat up in bed, and rubbed his eyes to dispel illusion. No. The chair was an ugly old gentleman; and what was more, he was winking at Tom Smart.

Charles Dickens, *Pickwick Papers*, 1837

Emma's mind was most busy, and, with all the wonderful velocity of thought, had been able . . . to see that Harriet's hopes had been entirely groundless, a mistake, a delusion, as complete delusion as any of her own.

Jane Austen, Emma, 1816

alternative, alternate

Both words can be nouns and adjectives, and are derived from the same Latin source *alternus* meaning 'every other' (from *alter* meaning 'other of two'). *Alternate* is also a verb (on which more below).

There is an important difference in meaning and usage of these two words. As a noun and adjective *alternative* refers to what is available as a different choice, as in *an alternative route home* (not the usual one) and *there is no alternative* (no other way or choice). Below are some fuller examples:

*Vice-chancellors are acting responsibly to find **alternative** sources of funding.*
*He's not fully committed yet. He may have an **alternative** up his sleeve.*
*We conclude by considering **alternatives** to the present system of local taxation.*

Alternate should not be used in this way in BrE:

✗ *In each moment of time countless trillions of **alternate** universes are sparked off.*

But note that this use of *alternate* is standard in AmE, so you will find it regularly in American sources:

*If the unexpected happens and the hotel is completely full and they have overbooked then it is the responsibility of the hotel to find **alternate** accommodation of the same standard at another hotel.*

In BrE, and in AmE, *alternate* means 'occurring by turns', first one then the other, of two or more things:

*Tone your breasts by spraying them with **alternate** bursts of warm and cold water then smooth on lots of body lotion.*
*In **alternate** weeks the auction is wholly devoted to domestic buyers or to foreign buyers.*

Alternate (with the stress on the first syllable) is also a verb meaning 'to interchange or take turns':

*It certainly keeps me on my toes as the children **alternate** between bouts of great industry and water fights.*

although, though

These two words are interchangeable as conjunctions that introduce a clause:

*Normally we could have a rudimentary shower using the plastic jug, **although** hot water wasn't often available.*
***Although** he was allowed visitors following his conviction, he is once again being denied visits.*

Note that *although* is more forceful and often preferable at the beginning of a sentence. But *though* alone can be used as an adverb in the middle or end of a sentence:

*Now **though** she only wanted to sit in her room a while.*
*Give him credit, **though**, he had fought his way to the top and made good.*

aluminium, aluminum

The first, with the stress on -*min*-, is BrE, and the second, with the stress on -*lum*- (pronounced -loom-), is AmE.

ambiguous, ambivalent

Ambivalent became a vogue word in the 1980s and although it has settled down somewhat it still intrudes on the territory properly belonging to *ambiguous*. As a general rule, statements and assertions can be *ambiguous* (i.e. have more than one possible meaning), and people can be *ambivalent* (uncertain or undecided on a particular point):

*He sought refuge in vague and **ambiguous** promises.*
*An **ambiguous** rule will carry much less weight than a specific one.*
*I understood that my mother was **ambivalent** about marriage.*
*At the moment, the public has a rather **ambivalent** attitude toward science.*

amend, emend

Both words have the meaning 'to change (something written or stated) as a correction or improvement'. *Amend* is the general word, and typically refers to legal documents, whereas *emend* is used in the special context of the wording or reading of texts:

*What is needed is for Parliament to **amend** the Act so that it explains exactly how far the rule-making powers go.*

*He suggests we **emend** Claudia's last message to include the words 'the universal spirit'.*

amiable, amicable

The two words are largely interchangeable in the meaning 'friendly and approachable': *amiable* is more typically used to describe people and their natures whereas *amicable* tends to describe attitudes, feelings, experiences, and above all decisions and actions, but the distinction is not clear-cut:

*It was rather cruel of me to take advantage of your **amiable** nature.*
*As far as I can make out Walter was an **amiable** scamp.*
*The Gnomes whiled away an **amiable** half hour telling anyone who would listen the entire history of the Crown Jewels.*

*The best course may be to seek an **amicable** parting of the ways.*
*We are still looking for an **amicable** solution to the problem.*
*All in all it could be said to have been an **amicable** evening.*

among, amongst

*The ducks bobbed and weaved **among** the rice shoots.*
*The River Inver, coming down **amongst** trees from the hills behind, has a pleasant path alongside.*

The two words are largely interchangeable, but *among* is about five times as common. They can refer both to physical position (as in the examples above) and to a notional place in a group (as in the examples below):

*Some universities, **among** them Cambridge, have extended their activities in this field.*
*They had a code name **amongst** themselves.*

Among and *amongst* are typically used with plural nouns, as in all the examples given so far. But both words are widely used with collective nouns that are grammatically singular but imply 'more than one' in various ways:

*There was an appalling lack of religious knowledge **amongst** the younger generation.*
*They are unique **among** the deer family in that both males and females have antlers which are eaten when shed.*
***Amongst** all the abuse, he especially valued a letter from Swinburne.*
*It is a deadly poison that will kill you if it gets in **among** the food.*

If the noun is distinctly singular or uncountable, it is usually better to use *amid* or *amidst* or *in the midst of*:

? *It was difficult to concentrate **amongst** [✓ amidst or in the midst of] all that noise.*

See also BETWEEN, AMONG.

amoral, immoral

These words are not interchangeable but each can often be used in place of the other without apparent error, so that the wrong meaning will be understood by anyone who knows the difference.

An *immoral* person or act or situation is one that offends against accepted morality:

*It's **immoral** to be rich when so many people are starving and homeless.*
***Immoral** private behaviour is no ground for dismissal.*

Amoral is typically applied to a person and means 'having no understanding of or concern with morals':

*We are forcing our teachers to become **amoral** dispensers of knowledge.*

In other words, *immorality* breaks a moral code, whereas *amorality* fails or refuses to recognize any moral code.

amount of, number of

When followed by *of, amount* typically refers to a mass of something uncountable, such as *sugar, money*, or *furniture*, or abstract concepts such as *energy, courage*, or *time*, and is a synonym of *quantity*, whereas *number of* is typically followed by a plural noun:

*It would be demeaning to wrangle over such a small **amount** of money.*
*Local authorities will need a substantial **amount** of time to ensure their information technology is correct.*
*The **number** of containers in the world is going to double.*

Note that *amount of* is followed by a plural noun to distinguish a collective meaning from an individual one:

*The world's waters differ greatly in the **amount** of minerals dissolved in them.*

In this sentence, replacing *amount* with *number* would signify the count of minerals (i.e. the range of different minerals) rather than their collective quantity.

amphitheatre

This is spelt *amphi-* (from Greek *amphi* meaning 'all around') and not (as often seen) *ampi-*. It refers to a type of ancient Roman theatre that forms a complete circle, like the Colosseum in Rome, that was used mainly for gladiatorial spectacles. It is not just a classier word for an ancient Greek or Roman theatre for drama, like the one at Epidaurus, which is open at one end where the stage is.

analogous

It properly means rather more than 'similar' or 'comparable'. It is the adjective based on *analogy*, which is a comparison made in order to clarify or explain, and should mean 'comparable in specific ways', i.e. ways that suggest an analogy:

*Such fissures were by no means peculiar to the middle classes of the Russian Empire: **analogous** divisions can be found throughout Europe.*

Note that *analogous* can be followed by *to* or (less usually) *with*:

The pinnacle of this endeavour currently is transplant surgery, or 'spare-part surgery', **analogous** to the replacement of worn-out parts in a machine.

*In being impressed by the certainty of the seen and the known one is assuming that seeing and knowing are **analogous** with looking and thinking.*

and

This is used informally instead of *to* with the verbs *come*, *go*, and *try*, typically in the imperative (as a command) and in statements in the future:

***Come and** see for yourself.*
*John will **come and** pick me up on Saturday.*
***Go and** fetch the corkscrew.*
*Shall we **try and** find them?*

Come and *go* (but not *try*) can also be used in the past in this way, with the verb following and also in the past:

*I **went and** saw them.*
*The police **came and** sealed off the street.*
*We **tried to** tell [✗ and told] you.*

anemone

The name of the plant is correctly spelt -*mone*, not -*nome*, although this is sometimes found. The word means 'wind flower' (from Latin *animus* 'wind'), because the flowers are said to open when there is a wind. This is a good way of remembering the correct spelling.

anonymous

Note the spelling with -*y*-. The noun is *anonymity*, with the stress on -nym-. The proper meaning has to do with a lack of name or identity:

*I'd like to have thanked him personally, but we have to respect his wish to remain **anonymous**.*
*Three **anonymous** articles appeared in an Aberdeen newspaper.*

A secondary meaning, 'having no distinctive or interesting features', has become well established:

*This new wave of **anonymous** buildings, designed to slip as quickly as possible through local authority planning procedures.*

This is a typical erosion or shift of meaning, but it is best to avoid uses that are counterintuitive or incongruous, e.g. where the notion of disguised identity does not work well:

*She was sitting in an **anonymous** hotel lobby in central London.*

anti-, ante-

These two prefixes, both derived from Latin words, have different meanings and it is important not to confuse them. The more common is *anti-* meaning 'against', which occurs in words such as *antibiotic, anticlerical, anticlimax, anticlockwise, antidepressant, anti-Semitism, antisocial*, and so on – all words to do with opposing or resisting something. It is an active suffix that can be used to form new words as needed (e.g. *anti-television, anti-waste*, and so on). In these ad hoc formations a hyphen is usual, especially in longer words. *Ante-*, on the other hand, means 'before' and forms words such as *antedeluvian* ('before the Flood'), *antenatal* ('before a birth'), *anteroom* ('a small room in front of a larger one'), and so on.

anticipate

Here is a word that causes a lot of trouble. Properly used, it should imply an element of forward thinking and 'forestalling' and not just 'expecting':

✓ *A skilful opponent can sometimes **anticipate** [= think ahead to (and prevent)] this move.*
✓ *These ideas **anticipated** [= looked forward to] Romanticism and had a profound effect on writers and artists.*

If you mean simply 'expect', use that word instead:

✗ *We **anticipate** [✓ expect] a large crowd this year.*
✗ *Everything is going as **anticipated** [✓ expected].*

> *In spring there will be a yellow dance, | they say, of daffodils and orchards, in this place | where what I anticipate most cheerfully is breakfast.*
>
> Maggie Anderson, *A Space Filled with Moving*, 1992

antisocial

See UNSOCIABLE, UNSOCIAL.

anyone, any one

Anyone (or *anybody*) is a pronoun meaning 'any person':

Anyone can make a planning application on any land even if they do not own the land.

As with *any*, *anyone* is used after a negative where *someone* would be used in a corresponding positive statement:

*I didn't tell **anyone** anything.*

Any one is written as two words when the separate meaning of the two words is intended, *any* usually being removable without disrupting the structure and usually without significantly altering the meaning:

*There may be twelve to eighteen places at **any one** of the drama schools.*
*There is a limit to the quantity of **any one** particular food you can eat without other foods.*
*The Rhine, Elbe, and Moselle are Germany's three greatest rivers, and a luxury cruise on **any one** of them is probably the best way of taking in the superb scenery.*

anyway, any way

Anyway is an adverb meaning 'in any case':

*Come with me. I'm going **anyway**.*

It is also used as a semi-conjunction in initial position to resume a narrative in the sense 'be that as it may' or 'whatever the case':

She laughed, as if to cover her outburst. '**Anyway,** *you're quite right.*'

Any way, like *any one*, is written as two words when the meaning is compositional and each word retains its own identity:

*They want to find out if there is **any way** [= any means or method] of predicting it and preventing it happening again.*
*There wasn't **any way** that [= any means by which] Evelyn could undo the damage.*
*She desired that the legacy should not be **in any way** [= in any respect or detail] altered by the pope nor any other person.*

apostrophes

The apostrophe has two main roles in modern punctuation:

• to indicate a possessive, as in *Carl's house* and *the city's main square.*
• to indicate omitted letters, as in *I'll wait for you* and *The train's late.*

Singular nouns form the possessive by adding *'s* (*the cat's bowl* = one cat), and plural nouns ending in *s* add an apostrophe after the *s* (*the cats' bowls* = more than one cat).

When a plural noun ends in a letter other than *s*, the possessive is formed by adding *'s*: *the children's shoes, the women's rooms, the people's complaints*, etc.

The infamous 'grocers' apostrophe', to be avoided at all costs in serious writing, is an apostrophe wrongly applied to an ordinary plural, particularly in words ending in *-o* but also in quite straightforward words such as *apple's* and *pear's* (e.g. *pear's 30p a pound*).

Beware also of confusing *who's* and *whose* (see the separate entry WHO'S AND WHOSE).

Names ending in *-s*, such as *Charles* and *Mars*, cause a special problem because of the awkward sound that can result when another *s* is added. Practice varies, but the best course is to add *'s* to names that end in *s* when you would pronounce the resulting form with an extra *s* in speech (e.g. *Charles's*, *Dickens's*, *Thomas's*, *The Times's*); and omit *'s* when the name is normally pronounced without the extra *s* (e.g. *Bridges'*, *Connors'*, *Mars'*, *Pericles'*). With French names ending in (silent) *-s* or *-x*, it is best to add *'s* (e.g. *Dumas's*, *le Roux's*) and then pronounce the possessive word with a final *-z*.

An apostrophe should not be used in the pronouns *hers*, *its*, *ours*, *yours*, and *theirs* (e.g. *an idea of yours* and *the house was theirs*). *Its* (as in *Remove the picture from its frame*) should also be distinguished from *it's* = 'it is' or 'it has' (as in *It's impossible to tell* and *It's been snowing*).

An apostrophe is no longer normally used in the plural of abbreviated forms (e.g. *several MPs were standing around*), although it is of course used in the possessive (e.g. *the BBC's decision to go ahead with the broadcast*). It is used in plurals when clarity calls for it, e.g. *dot your i's and cross your t's*. The apostrophe is also rapidly disappearing in company names and other commercial uses, e.g. *Lloyds Bank*, *Citizens Advice Bureau*.

The apostrophe is used to mark contractions such as *I've*, *we'll*, *wouldn't*, and *he's*, and informally also in contractions involving nouns (e.g. *The dinner's on the table*).

Apostrophes are no longer used to spell words that were originally contractions but are now treated as words in their own right, e.g. *cello*, *flu*, *phone*, and *plane*. A few words still have apostrophes in the middle for clarity, e.g. *fo'c'sle*, *ne'er-do-well*, *o'er*, *rock 'n' roll*.

appraise, apprise

These words are commonly confused: usually *appraise* is used when *apprise* is needed.

To *appraise* is to evaluate or assess:

*Let's **appraise** the pros and cons of the camera types we have mentioned.*
*The problem is obviously one of deciding how to **appraise** the evidence presented to us.*

To *apprise* is to inform, and is always followed by *of* referring to the matter being informed about:

*She should at least have taken a little time to **apprise** herself **of** the changing political situation.*
*An emissary would be permitted to leave Berwick to **apprise** the so-called Regent **of** this arrangement.*

Beware of the wrong use of *appraise*:

✗ *He looked around for someone to keep him **appraised** of [✓ apprised of or informed about] developments.*

apt, liable, prone

All three words are used to convey marked tendencies or habitual states or actions:

*As a London man, he was **apt to** be contemptuous of mere countryside.*
*Memories are **apt to** play tricks on us.*
*People are **liable to** continue to accept what they have been taught as young children.*
*Pedantic people are **prone to** point out minor typos and spelling mistakes.*

These examples show the typical pattern of following *apt*, *liable*, and *prone* with a *to*-infinitive, and in this construction the three words are largely interchangeable; but note that *apt* and *prone* tend to imply disapproval rather more than *liable*, which tends to emphasize the notion of responsibility.

Liable also has a special role in the context of legal obligation:

*Students **liable to** pay the higher rate of fee must apply concurrently for an award under the scheme.*

Liable to and *prone to*, but not *apt to*, can be followed by a simple noun object (in the case of *prone to*, including an *-ing* verb which acts as a noun) instead of a *to*-clause:

*She is **liable to** spells of nervous depression.*
*Profits made by a parents' association are **liable to** taxation.*
*Being a Celt, I am **prone to** moods.*
*Spray bottles are particulary **prone to** misuse.*

*He was still **prone to** falling head-over-heels in love with young women.*

It is worth remembering that *likely to* can be a better choice when referring to a particular or immediate probability rather than a more general tendency or possibility:

*If you always follow the same procedure, you are less **likely to** make mistakes.*
*These costs are **likely to** be hefty in the next few years.*

Arab, Arabic, Arabian

Arab is the word for a member of the people called *Arabs*, inhabiting parts of the Middle East and North Africa, and is also used as an adjective, as in *Arab students, the Arab world*. *Arabic* is the name (noun and adjective) of the language. *Arabian* is a geographical term, as in *the Arabian sands* and *the Arabian peninsula*, and is also used historically in titles such as *The Arabian Nights*. The *Arabic numerals* are the figures 1, 2, 3, 4, 5, etc.

arbiter, arbitrator

The two words come from the same Latin root *arbiter* meaning 'judge', but there is an important difference in their meaning. An *arbiter* is 'a person or agency with absolute power of judging and determining', as in *an arbiter of fashion* or *taste*, someone who greatly influences the fashions or tastes of others. An *arbitrator* is someone appointed to arbitrate in a dispute, i.e. to decide in favour of one side or the other.

> *The taste and feelings of individuals must be the*
> *arbiters of their happiness.*
>
> Maria Edgeworth, *Belinda*, 1801

aren't

This contracted form of *are not* is unexceptionable in-formally in uses where *are not* would be legitimate as the full form, i.e. *we aren't, aren't you, they aren't,* and so on. More problematic is the form *aren't I* (typically used in questions), which is a poorly formed twentieth-century contraction: *aren't I right about that?* It is more widely condemned in American usage guides than in British, but the alternative *am I not* is much to be preferred.

Argentina, Argentine, Argentinian

The correct name of the South American country is *Argentina,* not now *the Argentine.* A person from Argentina is an *Argentinian,* which is also the form of the adjective (as in ✓ *the Argentinian navy,* not ✗ *the Argentine navy*).

as

Two special uses of *as* are worth noting. They both concern its role as a conjunction (i.e. to introduce a clause with a verb).

- **as = 'because'**

In this meaning, *as* tends to be more effective when it comes at the beginning of the sentence:

As he only laughed at my arguments, I gave it up.

When the order is reversed, *since* is often better (and in this order the emphasis on the clause containing the reason is stronger):

I gave it up, since he only laughed at my arguments.

- **as = 'though'**

As can be used in place of *though* in constructions such as *much as I like them* and *good as they may look*, in which a contrary statement follows: *much as I like them I cannot afford to buy them.* The American practice of adding an initial *as* (in the manner of a comparison) is spreading into British use, but it is strictly redundant and can even be confusing:

As old-fashioned as the performance sounded at times, it was undeniably moving and deeply satisfying.

ascent, assent

An *ascent* is a movement upwards (*the ascent of the North Face*); *assent* is a noun meaning 'permission or approval' (as in *to give one's assent*) and a verb meaning 'to agree (to)' (as in *assented to the proposal*).

assassin, assassinate, assassination

These gruesome words are each spelt with two sets of *-ss-*. The word is related to *hashish*: the original Assassins were a fanatical Muslim sect at the time of the Crusades, who used hashish before embarking on murder missions.

assent

See ASCENT, ASSENT.

assignment, assignation

These two words, both derivatives of the verb *assign*, share the meaning 'the act of or an instance of assigning':

*Measures taken include the **assignment** of two junior ministers to the Security Ministry.*
*Protagoras found gender **assignation** in Greek inconsistent and illogical.*

Each has a special meaning not shared by the other. An *assignment* can mean 'a task allocated to someone', typically a piece of work given to a student to do; and an *assignation* can mean 'a secret meeting, especially between lovers':

*We don't want her thinking that you and I made a secret **assignation** in Piccadilly Circus.*

assume, presume

Both words broadly mean 'suppose' and are to a large extent interchangeable; it is, however, useful to maintain a distinction, preferring *assume* in the sense of stating a hypothesis and *presume* in the sense of drawing a conclusion from evidence:

*We **assume** you can load and configure your own software.*

It seems reasonable to **assume** *that the animal started growing as a coiled shell.*

The audience is **assumed** *to hold similar views to the speaker's.*

You go to the weekly briefings. I **presume** *you were at this morning's?*

I hadn't even noticed the pickets and can only **presume** *that they had parted before me as I walked towards them.*

The king's wars were **presumed** *to be for the sake of peace.*

Note from the above examples that both words can be used with a simple object, a *that*-clause (or one with *that* omitted), or an object followed by a *to*-infinitive.

assure, ensure, insure

All three words have meanings to do with making safe or certain. To *assure* someone of something, or that something is so (with the option of omitting *that* in the clause), is to give them an assurance or undertaking that it is the case, has been or will be done, etc.:

'I'm very keen on tennis,' she **assured** *them earnestly.*

For our part, we **assure** *him* **of** *our loyal support.*

British Waterways **assure** *me something will be done about it.*

Physically handicapped students may be **assured that** *their applications will be considered.*

Ensure is used in the sense 'to make certain' and can be followed by a noun or a *that*-clause:

Systems were established to **ensure** *accuracy of information.*

All sperm is tested twice to **ensure that** *there has not been an error in the initial testing.*

Insure has the special meaning 'to take out insurance on *or* for' and is not a synonym of *ensure*:

*We will **insure** you against legal liability.*
*The car is economical to run and cheap to **insure**.*
✗ *I will do all I can to **insure** [✓ ensure or make sure] it doesn't happen again.*

-asy

See -ACY, -ASY.

atheist

See AGNOSTIC, ATHEIST.

aural, oral

These words describe related phenomena about things heard and said, one to do with the ear and hearing (*aural*, from Latin *auris* 'ear') and the other to do with the mouth and speaking (*oral*, from Latin *os, oris* 'mouth'):

*The words have subordinated the music to the level of glossy paper. Maybe people genuinely like their kind of **aural** semolina.*
***Oral** hygiene is vitally important.*

Because of the special role of the mouth in speaking, *oral* has the extended meaning 'spoken, using speech (as distinct from writing)':

*It was perhaps originally an **oral** message from Cnut, committed to writing by an ecclesiastic for circulation.*

See also ORAL, VERBAL.

authoritarian, authoritative

Authoritarian is a pejorative (disapproving) word meaning 'domineering or tyrannical':

*The **authoritarian** nature of the regime has won it many enemies both inside and outside the country.*
*The government's response was to resort to more **authoritarian** methods of policing the villages.*

Authoritative is a complimentary word meaning 'based on authority, definitive, conclusive':

*Reference librarians will tell you the most **authoritative** books on each subject.*
*The Bible began to be read with eyes no longer focused by the **authoritative** teaching of the Church.*

avenge, revenge

These two words are concerned with the same circumstances of seeking vengeance, but their uses differ. *Avenge* is the more common word: you *avenge* someone (including yourself) for a wrong or suffering, or you *avenge* the act itself, whereas you *revenge* only an act or (more typically) yourself, and you can also *be revenged on* someone when that someone is the object of your revenge:

*Her aim was to **avenge** the brutal treatment of comrades in police custody.*
*In time, perhaps, these deaths will **be avenged**.*

*Authors are not supposed to **avenge** themselves in their writing.*
*Have you come to **revenge** yourself on me for failing you?*
*I have often thought, like Malvolio, that I will **be revenged** on the whole pack of you.*

Revenge is more commonly used as a noun, and *to take* (or *seek*) *revenge on someone* (or *for something*) conveniently covers most cases:

*It is difficult to take **revenge on** someone you cannot picture.*
*A king would come from Asia to seek **revenge for** what the Romans had done to the Greeks.*

averse

See ADVERSE, AVERSE.

avert, avoid, evade

These three words all have to do with refraining or preventing and therefore overlap in meaning, but they have important differences.

Avoid is by far the most common word and has two main meanings: (1) to prevent oneself from unwanted contact (with a person, thing, or situation), and (2) to act in a way that prevents a consequence (invariably an unpleasant or unwelcome one). The grammatical object can be either a simple noun or a phrase introduced by an *-ing* verb:

*Pearce had a constant battle to **avoid** bankruptcy.*
*The especially important thing is to **avoid** cheese at night.*
*Prey becomes better equipped to **avoid** being killed.*

*I could not **avoid** him, since we had to play together.*

Evade has a similar meaning to *avoid*, and typically applies to a duty or commitment with the implication of guile or trickery:

*He **evaded** arrest and escaped to Norway.*
*Hooligans often take care to **evade** police escorts and slip into rival territories.*
*There was no point in **evading** the issue any longer.*

Avert tends to retain more directly its etymological sense (from Latin *avertere*) of 'turning aside or away' and is typically used of something unpleasant or harmful, rather than avoiding in the sense of steering oneself around or away from an obstacle or danger:

*Eventually, the crew were paid and a crisis **averted**.*
*They had exhausted existing ways of **averting** ethnic conflict.*

Note that unlike *avoid*, *evade* is less commonly used with an *-ing* verb and *avert* cannot be used with one:

? *If he could have **evaded** [better: avoided] meeting the poor man even for a few days, the squabble could have been settled.*

USAGE NOTE – To *avert your eye* (or *gaze*) is to look away from a person or thing you do not want to see; to *avoid a person's eye* is not to look at them so that they do not look at you.

awesome

Awesome is spelt with an *e* in the middle (from *awe* meaning 'wonder'). It properly means 'evoking wonder' (as in *an awesome sight*), but it has developed an informal meaning that is little more than 'excellent' or 'wonderful' (rather like *terrific* and *wicked*), and you need to be aware of this when using it in more formal writing.

> *Anger made her beauty awesome. | From her full height she raked the worshippers | With a glare of contempt.*
>
> Ted Hughes, *Tales from Ovid*, 1997

awfully, dreadfully, incredibly, terribly

*The man's eyes flashed and he looked **awfully** annoyed.*
*They left him feeling **dreadfully** depressed.*
*It is a lightweight yet **incredibly** powerful machine.*
*It is **terribly** important for people to have proper training.*

Adverbs of this type have become so weakened in force as to mean little more than 'very' or 'extremely'. They play a useful role as intensifying words adding colour to everyday conversation, and it would be difficult to avoid them completely, but there are often better words available that make more impact in writing, such as *extremely* or *exceedingly*, or (especially when describing feelings and emotions) *intensely* and *acutely*. In many cases, *very* is quite adequate:

*The man's eyes flashed and he looked **intensely** annoyed.*
*They left him feeling **acutely** depressed.*

*It is a lightweight yet **extremely** powerful machine.*
*It is **very** important for people to have proper training.*

This topic is discussed more fully in *How to Write Better English*, pp. 143–6.

backward, backwards, *and related words*

In BrE *backward* and similar words such as *downward, forward, homeward, northward,* etc. are the more usual forms than the corresponding forms ending in *-wards* when they are adjectives (as in *a backward glance, a downward trend, a forward movement, the northward carriageway,* etc.). The forms *backwards* etc. are more usual when they are adverbs, i.e. when they qualify verbs (as in *glancing backwards, driving homewards, turning northwards, etc.*):

*The Post Office warned that it was a **backward** step which could hit local mail deliveries.*
*The man had mistaken a road to his right for the **southward** lane of a dual carriageway.*
*Little was said on the **homeward** journey.*
*Give the handle a sharp **downward** pull.*
*On and on went the machines, **backwards** and **forwards**, **backwards** and **forwards**.*
***Eastwards** are the ruins of the Chapel of St Mary.*
*During the Turkish occupation, many Serbs migrated **northwards** across the Danube.*
*She got into her car and pointed it **homewards**.*

Adverb forms in *-ward* are more common in AmE and are also found in BrE:

*The woman was on him like a tigress, pulling him **backward** by his hair.*
*The main street sweeps **southward** up the hill.*
*The sun was setting as the rector set off **homeward**.*
*'Backspace' moves the cursor **backward** to the previous input field.*

Avoid inconsistency of the kind found in the following example:

? *As you move both hands **forward** or **backwards** which arm takes more weight?*

bacteria

Note that this is a plural noun: *The bacteria are [✗ is] found naturally in a person's nose.*

bail, bale

Both words exist as a noun and verb, and the forms overlap in usage. *Bail* is money paid to a court to secure a person's temporary release, and *to bail someone out* is an idiom based on this, meaning 'to rescue someone from a difficulty or danger'. In the plural, *bails* are the small crosspieces that lie on top of the stumps in cricket. A *bale* is a bundle of paper, hay, or cotton, and the verb *to bale* (or *bale out*) means to scoop water out of a boat. *To bale out* also means 'to make a parachute jump from an aircraft in an emergency'. In AmE, *bail* is preferred in these verb senses, and this spelling is used as well as *bale* in BrE.

baited, bated

Baited is the past and past participial form of the verb *bait* meaning 'to tease or provoke cruelly' and also 'to put bait in a trap'. The phrase *with bated breath* means 'in agitated suspense', and the spelling here is *bated*: it comes from an old verb *bate* meaning 'to reduce in size or strength', which is what you do to your breath when you hold it.

baleful, baneful

Because they are not used all that often, these words are easily confused. *Baleful* means 'deadly or menacing' and is typically used with words such as *look*, *glare*, *stare*, etc. *Baneful* is related to *bane* (as in *the bane of their lives*) and means 'harmful' (as in *a baneful influence*).

barely, hardly, scarcely

These restrictive adverbs are largely interchangeable when used with adjectives and verbs:

*The shapes in the room were **barely** discernible.*
*The cubicles just had curtains which **barely** covered the openings.*
*There's **hardly** any snow here.*
*Charles was **hardly** noticed.*
*He invited the young man, **scarcely** more than a boy, to be his private secretary.*
*She could **scarcely** complain.*

If the sentence continues with some kind of event clause, this should be introduced by a time word such as *when* or *before* and not *than*:

*Filming had **barely** started **when** stories began to circulate about Lazenby's difficult behaviour.*
*The ink was **hardly** dry on the takeover agreement **when** he made his first inept move against me.*
*She and D'Arcy had **scarcely** dismounted **before** the door swung open.*

If the adverb starts the sentence, the verb and subject are turned round by a process called 'inversion':

***Hardly** had Harry finished imparting this encouraging news **when** Miriam returned.*

> *Scarcely had we made our bows, and shaken our hands, and imparted our observations about the fineness of the weather, when behold! as we look from the drawing-room windows into the cheerful square of Bryanstone, a great family coach arrives, driven by a family coachman in a family wig, and we recognise Lady Ann Newcome's carriage, and see her ladyship, her mother, her daughter, and her husband, Sir Brian, descend from the vehicle.*
>
> William Thackeray, *The Newcomes*, 1854

based on

Avoid using *based on* as an unattached conjunction without a clear antecedent:

✗ *The situation will be evaluated **based on** [✓ according to] these criteria.*

This is especially important when *based on* comes at the beginning of the sentence:

✗ ***Based on*** [✓ *In accordance with*] *our new policy, I'd suggest the following . . .*

The illogical alternative *based around* should also be avoided:

✗ *Training should be **based around** a community or project need.*

basically

Basically has a core or nominal meaning 'as a fundamental fact or set of facts', and is synonymous with *essentially* and *fundamentally*:

*There are **basically** four elements required before a system can even begin to be considered as a desktop publishing tool.*

Because of its very generalized meaning it tends to be used as a redundant filler:

*You strike me as a **basically** good-natured and decent girl.*
*Five years on, their marriage ended. '**Basically**, I was bored.'*
*You know, **basically**, by and large, we don't know.*

This informal usage, though useful in conversation, is best avoided in important or formal writing.

basis

The phrase *on a – basis* has a useful role:

*Profit levels can be more accurately assessed **on a job-by-job basis**.*

This is a more precise and better focused way of expressing the point than by saying, for example, *profit levels can be more accurately assessed job by job*.

The formula is also useful when there is already another adverb ending in *-ally* immediately preceding:

*All salaries are reviewed periodically, normally **on an annual basis**.* (*. . . normally annually* is grammatically sound, but a little awkward.)

But there is little point in using the phrase to pad out simple adverbs that are just as effective by themselves:

? *The formula ensures that shareholders are treated **on an equal basis**.*
   (✓ *. . . are treated **equally***)
? *Fees for longer or shorter courses are calculated **on a pro rata basis**.*
   (✓ *. . . are calculated **pro rata***)

bated

See BAITED, BATED.

bath, bathe

The uses of these two related words overlap in the verb meaning 'to take a bath', which can be either *bath* or *bathe* though more usually the former. To *bathe* is now more usually understood as swimming in the sea or in a swimming bath. You can also *bath* someone (= give them a bath) and *bathe* a wound (= clean it with water). The normal noun is *bath*, both for the object and for the act of taking a bath, but *bathe* is used as a noun in the sense 'an act or spell of bathing' (*went for a bathe*), especially in the sea.

because

Be careful to avoid the following kind of ambiguity when *because* comes after a negative statement:

*They did not want to leave **because** there was work to be done.*

This could mean either (1) they wanted to stay to get on with the work, or (2) they wanted to leave but not to avoid doing the work. If the meaning intended is the first one, a comma after *leave* will clarify this, and if it is the second, the order of the sentence should be reversed to express this more clearly:

(1) *They did not want to leave, **because** there was work to be done.*
(An alternative is to avoid the negative altogether: *They wanted to stay **because** there was work to be done.*)
(2) *It was not **because** there was work to be done that they wanted to leave.*
(An alternative is *They wanted to leave, but not **because** there was work to be done.*)

See also REASON IS . . .

beg the question

This expression taken from the language of logical argument properly means 'to assume as true what the argument is setting out to prove to be true':

*The notion that aggression is a given characteristic in humans everywhere **begs the question** and determines the formulation of the research.*
(Because this is the point being investigated.)

It tends to be used to express other meanings for which good alternatives are available:

- 'to suggest or give rise to the question':

✗ *Palin cannot bear to be criticized. Which rather **begs the question** [✓ raises the question] why he became an actor.*

- 'to evade the issue; to duck the question':

✗ *This approach **begs the question** [✓ evades the issue] by failing to provide an answer to the main issue.*

behalf

On behalf of means 'in the interests of' or 'for the benefit of' or 'as a representative of':

✓ *Clive would go on fighting **on behalf of** [= in the interests of] the workers.*
✓ *It is not known what arrangements were made **on the players' behalf** [= for their benefit].*
✓ *He remained concerned over the claims of the NUS to speak **on behalf of** [= as representative of] individual students.*

It does not properly mean 'on the part of' and should not be used in this sense:

✗ *A little bit of anger **on their own behalf** [✓ on their part] would be a very positive thing.*

✗ *There is a lot of new interest generated **on behalf of** [✓ on the part of, by] journalists.*

beside, besides

As a preposition, *beside* means 'next to at the side' (*the path beside the church*) and, in a figurative sense, 'compared with' (*seems cheap beside its competitors*). *Besides* means 'apart from' or 'in addition to' (*hoping to find something besides rubbish / understood the meanings besides being able to spell the words*). *Besides* is also an adverb in the sense 'in any case' (*And besides, they had only just met*).

between, among

The physical meaning of *between* in relation to physical measurement and distance – normally involving two places or points – has given rise to the notion that in abstract senses it can only be used when two people or things are involved. This is a misconception that fails to understand the way uses develop in more ways than one (i.e. not only in meaning): in fact, use of *between* with reference to more than two things is common and often preferable to the proposed alternative *among* (or *amongst*: see the entry for these words above):

*These dense clouds **between** the stars have temperatures ten degrees above absolute zero.*
*Consider using strips of black polythene **between** rows to reduce the need for watering in a good summer.*

*This exchange of knowledge is a pathway to better understanding **between** nations.*
*Where information is adequate from the poorest nations it points to a close relationship **between** poverty, underdevelopment, and the spread of Aids.*

between you and me

Since both pronouns are governed by the preposition *between*, this is the correct grammar: not ✗ *between you and I*. The same applies to other prepositions, such as *for*, *of*, *to*, and *with*, and to other pronouns, e.g. *her*, *him*, *them*, *us*.

That is for you and him to decide.
This is a photo of Sadie and her.

You can readily see the grammatical logic if you simplify each sentence to contain just the pronoun:

That is for him [✗ he] to decide.
This is a photo of her [✗ she].

biennial, biannual

Biennial means 'once every two years' and *biannual* means 'twice a year': so the difference is fourfold. If you think your readers might be unsure of the meaning in either case, it is better to use *alternate-year* instead of *biennial* (or rephrase in some way, e.g. 'appearing every other year'), and *twice-yearly* instead of *biannual*.

billion, trillion

In current BrE and AmE, a *billion* is a thousand million. The term for a million million, which in BrE used to be *billion*, is now *trillion*.

bipolar disorder

This term, which came into medical use in the 1970s, is now preferred to *manic depression*.

blanch, blench

Blanch is a mainly transitive verb (i.e. it takes a grammatical object) meaning 'to take the colour out of (something); to make pale':

*Earth up the stems of leeks and trench celery to **blanch** them.*
*Their cheeks were **blanched** and drawn as the party set out in the driving rain.*

It has a special meaning in cookery, 'to scald or parboil (especially almonds)', and can also be used intransitively (without an object) with the thing that becomes pale as the subject instead of the object:

*He saw her **blanch** and veil her eyes.*
*Elinor **blanched**, her pallor more obvious against her peach chiffon robe.*

Blench is an intransitive verb meaning 'to shrink in fear':

*Many rational people, who would walk under a ladder without **blenching**, back surreptitiously away from making a will.*

The two words come close in meaning, and are almost interchangeable, when denoting reactions of alarm, horror, dismay, etc:

He used to add that my handbags would make a strong man **blench**.

People who have children may **blanch** *at the idea of those cream sofas.*

It is important, however, to be aware of the somewhat differing literal image suggested by these uses.

blatant, flagrant

Blatant was coined by the Elizabethan poet Edmund Spenser, and in modern use means 'completely obvious or conspicuous', normally in the context of disapproval:

Staff claim they were shocked by her **blatant** *flirting and hand-holding.*

This was an example of judicial creativity at its most **blatant**.

In a **blatant** *appeal to the constituency's Roman Catholic vote, the Labour candidate appears on the ballot paper as 'Pope, Gregory'.*

In nineteenth-century literature, *blatant* was typically used to describe people themselves rather than their behaviour:

> *O, I know he's a good fellow – you needn't frown – an*
> *excellent fellow, and I always mean to see more of him;*
> *but a hide-bound pedant for all that; an ignorant,*
> *blatant pedant.*

> R. L. Stevenson, *The Strange Case of Dr Jekyll and Mr Hyde*, 1886

Flagrant is an older word that is broadly similar in meaning, but with a stronger emphasis on the offensive or shocking nature of the act it describes than on its obviousness or incontrovertibility:

*Kim's **flagrant** disobedience earlier that evening had caused him acute public embarrassment.*

*In a **flagrant** breach of Victorian morality he persuaded his inamorata, Elspeth Thomson, to follow him down to Cornwall and into a whirlwind marriage.*

*The ill doings of his family and associates were **flagrant** enough to bring about a fatal confrontation.*

The same distinction applies to the adverbial forms *blatantly* (much the more common word) and *flagrantly*:

*How could any red-blooded male ignore the message the actress was sending so **blatantly**?*

*He was jailed for 30 years after a **blatantly** unfair trial.*

*Some species of spider will **blatantly** mimic the 'come-hither' sound signals and even sex pheromones of female moths.*

*You have obviously tried not to plagiarize too **flagrantly**.*

*Is it not clear that our MPs have **flagrantly** broken the declared policy of the Party?*

Use of the adverb *blatantly* in its more recent weakened meaning equivalent to 'absolutely' or 'extremely', in contexts not involving displays of behaviour or feeling, is best kept for informal conversation:

? *Blatantly they weren't going to agree to that.*

blog

Blog, a personal website on the Internet, is a shortening like *cello*. The full form is *weblog*, but this, like *violoncello*, is the preserve of formal documents and manuals. A person who has a blog is *a blogger*, and the activity is called *blogging*.

bored

✘ *When we got bored of the clubs, we would go to the beach.*

The adjectival form *bored* should be followed by *with* and not (as above) *of* (which has come on the scene partly on the analogy of *tired of* and partly because in rapid speech *with* starts to sound like *of*).

both . . . and . . .

*Mr Elliott suffered **both** internal **and** external injuries when he was allegedly run down twice by a car.*

When used as an adverb as in the above example, *both* should be paired with *and* and not *or*, and it is important to balance the two parts of the structure:

*I do admit to being **both** baffled **and** intrigued.*
*There is an obvious mixture of pointers **both** for **and** against the existence of A Deity.*
*The segregation of the sexes in paid employment may be considered to have **both** a vertical **and** a horizontal component.*

Avoid an inconsistent balance of the *both . . . and . . .* structure as illustrated by the following sentences:

✗ *Older brides were often preferred, as they tended to be **both** more useful as work partners, and have fewer childbearing years before them.*

(Reorder as ✓ *. . . tended **both** to be more useful as work partners, and to have fewer childbearing years before them . . .,* or rephrase as ✓ *. . . tended to be **both** more useful as work partners, and likely to have fewer childbearing years before them,* making the two parts balance.)

✗ *The war has accentuated the disparities **both** in educational level and general economic status between different regions of the country.*

(There needs to be another *in* after *and* to balance the first *in*: ✓ *The war has accentuated the disparities **both** in educational level and in general economic status.* Alternatively, make the first *in* govern the two parts: ✓ *The war has accentuated the disparities in **both** educational level and general economic status.*)

both, both of

Both can be used as a modifying word or as a kind of pronoun followed by *of*. The first choice emphasizes the combination of people or things and the second choice emphasizes their individuality:

*He gripped **both** her arms, lifting and pulling.*
*Life has been good to **both of** us since we came to Swinbrook.*
(Or you could say . . . *to us both* . . .)
*We **both** read them and we **both** made the same mistake.*
***Both** parents came of established farming families.*

It is easy to fall into the trap of using *both* in ways that on reflection are illogical or even nonsensical:

? *There is a fuse in **both** sections of the circuit.*

What the writer of this sentence meant was that there are two fuses, one in each section of the circuit. There is nothing grammatically wrong with the sentence but it is plainly illogical since a single fuse cannot be in two points at once. This sentence therefore needs either to be put in the plural or to be recast with *each* instead of *both*:

? *There are fuses in **both** sections of the circuit.*
(But this doesn't make it clear that there are only two.)
✓ *There is a fuse in **each** section of the circuit.*

breach, breech

A *breach* is a break or gap in a wall or fortification, but it is mostly used in figurative senses of a break in relations or a violation of a law or agreement (as in *breach of contract*). A *breech* is the part of a firearm near the rear end of the barrel, and in the plural *breeches* is a term for knee-length trousers that are closely fastened at the lower edges.

broach, brooch

Broach is a verb meaning 'to raise (a sensitive matter)':

*He **broached** the idea of bringing Anthony to his mother's next party.*

Brooch is a noun, a word for a piece of jewellery with a closable pin worn on clothing.

budget

Because the stress is on the first syllable, the verb *budget* has the inflections *budgeted* and *budgeting* (single *t* in each case).

bulk of

The noun phrase *the bulk of* should normally be followed by a singular uncountable noun (i.e. one that has no plural):

*Activities in number and language occupied **the bulk of** the children's time in school.*

It is poor style to use *the bulk of* with a plural noun; in this case use *the majority of* or (more simply) *most*:

✗ ***The bulk*** [✓ *Most* or *The majority*] ***of*** *her household goods had been settled earlier on her daughters.*

See also MAJORITY OF.

bus

The plural of the noun is *buses*. The verb, meaning 'to take someone by bus', typically used of taking school-children to a school in another part of town, is *bused* and *busing*, although *bussed* and *bussing* are permitted variants.

caffeine

Caffeine, the stimulant compound, is spelt -ei- and not -ie. It is an exception (like *protein*) to the rule *i* before *e* except after *c* (when pronounced -ee-).

calendar, colander

The first (from Latin *calendae*) is a list of dates, and the second (from Latin *colare* to sieve) is an implement for washing or draining food.

can, may

Can is used to express (1) possibility (*Anyone can make a mistake / It can often rain at this time of year*), (2) ability or capacity (*The virus can damage the immune system*), and (3) permission (*You can give my name as a referee*). In all these areas *may* is also used, least idiomatically in the first but more so in the second (*The virus may damage the immune system*) and third (*You may give my name as a referee*). The most controversial area is the third, in which *may* is traditionally more dominant and *can* seems to be (or is perceived as being) the intruder. The reason for this intrusion, however, is that the boundary between senses is not always clear-cut, so that an element of possibility or of ability or capacity may be present even when the predominant sense is one of permission. Usually, the broader context, or in speech the tone of voice, helps to identify the intended meaning.

The current situation is that in general usage *can* and

may are largely interchangeable in contexts involving permission, despite the occasional objections of language purists (which writers should be aware of). In more formal or polite contexts, *may* is preferable and more usual:

*You **may** leave now.*
***May** I have some tea, please?*

In the past tense, *could* has largely replaced *might* (which is the past form of *may*):

*In those days only registered readers **could** [= were entitled to] use the reading room.*

In some cases, a distinction between *can* and *may* needs to be preserved:

*If I **can** phone you it will be a lot easier [= if I am able, if I have the time, etc.].*
*If I **may** phone you it will be a lot easier [= if you will permit me, if that is convenient for you, etc.].*

There is notional ambiguity in the following types, although this tends to be more theoretical than actual:

*Students **may** use these facilities outside working hours [? = it is possible that students will use them: but may be using would be more idiomatic].*
*Students **can** use these facilities outside working hours [= students are allowed to use them].*

In practice, *may* is the more likely choice even though *can* is strictly speaking less ambiguous.

cancel

The verb doubles the final *l* in inflection (*cancelled*, *cancelling*) and in the derivative noun *cancellation*.

canoe

As a verb, this has the inflected forms *canoes*, *canoed*, *canoeing*.

canvas, canvass

Canvas with one *s* is a type of coarse cloth or a piece of this, and the plural is *canvases*. It is occasionally used as a verb in the sense 'to cover or line with canvas', and this doubles the final *s* in inflection (*canvasses*, *canvassed*, *canvassing*). *Canvass* with two *s*'s is a verb meaning 'to seek votes or opinions', which has the same set of inflections as *canvas*.

capability

See ABILITY, CAPABILITY, CAPACITY.

capital, capitol

The *capital* of a country or region is its most important town or city (London, Paris, Tokyo, Buenos Aires, etc.). This should be distinguished from *Capitol*, which is the hill in Rome saved by the geese, and an American legislative building, most famously the one in Washington DC.

capsize

Capsize, meaning 'to overturn a boat in the water', is one of those verbs ending in *-ize* that cannot also be spelt *-ise*. This is because the ending is not the (variable) suffix *-ize/-ise*. The origin of the word is uncertain, but it may be derived from Spanish *capuzar* meaning 'to sink a ship by its head' (from *cabo* 'head').

carburettor

The word for the fuel-mixing device in an internal-combustion engine is spelt *-ettor* in BrE (with a variant *-etter*). In AmE the spelling is *carburetor*.

Caribbean

The name for the region south of the Bahamas is spelt with one *r* and two *b*'s. It is pronounced with a stress on the third syllable in BrE, and on the second syllable in AmE.

carol, carrel

A *carol* is a seasonal hymn or song, especially one sung at Christmas. The less commonly used word *carrel* is a private cubicle for study in a library. The words are related in origin, both being derived from the Middle English word *carole* meaning 'a round dance' or 'ring'.

carousal, carousel

The two words have different origins. *Carousal* (pronounced ka-**rou**-zal) is a noun from *carouse* (ultimately from German *gar aus trinken* 'to drink all out') and means 'a drunken revel'. A *carousel* (pronounced ka-roo-**sel**) is a merry-go-round or, perhaps more commonly now, a rotating band that delivers luggage (if you are lucky) at an airport.

caster, castor

There is much confuson about which spelling to use for various things, partly arising from unstable usage. The recommendation here is to use *castor* for the small swivelled wheel mounted beneath a piece of furniture and for *castor oil*, and *caster* for the fine white type of sugar (originally kept in a pot called a *caster*).

catchphrases

These are phrases that 'catch on' very quickly and are constantly repeated. They usually have a specific and traceable origin (though not always). Their meanings are often not transparent but derived from the context of their origin. Examples are *not tonight, Josephine* (attributed to Napoleon but more likely a nineteenth-century music hall invention); *and so to bed* (from the concluding statement of diary entries of Samuel Pepys in the 1660s); more recently *and now for something completely different*, which originated in the early 1970s British comedy programme *Monty Python's Flying*

Circus; *go ahead, make my day* (an ironic form of challenge), based on a line spoken by Clint Eastwood in the 1983 film *Sudden Impact*, and *naughty but nice*, which originated in an advertising campaign to sell cream cakes in the 1980s. The New Zealand lexicographer Eric Partridge compiled a dictionary of catchphrases, published in 1977 (second edition, 1985). They are fine in their place (such as casual conversation) but, like clichés, can have a hackneyed and insincere effect that is not suitable in more serious writing.

cater

To cater *for* people or needs is the more usual construction; *cater to* (on the analogy of *pander to*) is going out of use except in AmE, and is restricted to impersonal objects:

*It is a clean and well-run campsite that **caters** only **for** families and couples.*
*The private tuition service is meeting a need that universities fail to **cater for**.*
*The winning recipe **caters to** what animals actually like – offal.*

cease, stop

Henry Fowler, author of the famous *Dictionary of Modern English Usage* (1926), wrote of *cease* that 'we substitute it for *stop* when we want our language to be dignified' and that 'no effort should be made to keep words of this kind at work'. To avoid appearances of pretentiousness, except in formal or technical contexts or for dramatic effect, it is better to use *stop*.

The players remained in their seats, waiting for the rain to **cease**.

Note that *cease* can be followed by a *to*-infinitive as well as an *-ing* verbal noun, whereas *stop* can only be followed by an *-ing* word:

If the current trend of losing manufacturing jobs continues at the present rate, then manufacturing will **cease** *to exist in 2029.*

(You would have to say *stop existing*, but this would be unidiomatic and would be replaced by a single word such as *discontinue*.)

censer, censor, censure

A *censer* is a container for incense (to which word it is related), and a *censor* is an official who judges the suitability of public entertainments (especially cinema films) for various age groups (or, in more sinister environments, cuts controversial material from personal letters). *Censure* is harsh criticism or open disapproval. To *censor* something is to be a censor of it; to *censure* someone is to criticize them harshly.

A telly show about jazz and classical music has been banned by the **censors**. *They said it had too much sax and violins.*
Why can't we **censor** *the images that are produced, removing them from the Internet, before they reach their intended audience?*
The regulator has warned broadcasters that they could face **censure** *if they show cartoons in which smoking is 'encouraged, glamorised, or condoned'.*

*A posthumous pardon implicitly **censures** one group of dead people – those who administered the justice we now seek to overturn – and rewards another, the accused soldiers.*

ceremonial, ceremonious

Ceremonial is a purely descriptive word meaning 'marked by or used in ceremony' (as in *a ceremonial occasion, a ceremonial mace*), whereas *ceremonious* is a judgemental word implying disapproval of excessive formality or punctiliousness:

✓ *The mayor, teachers, parents, friends and bank staff joined together for the **ceremonial** cutting of the ribbon.*
✓ *The writer was a diffident, **ceremonious** man unlikely to risk suggestive remarks to his upright publisher, Edward Arnold.*
✗ *The Councillor declared the urinals officially open and cut a **ceremonious** [✓ ceremonial] piece of loo roll, which had been hung across the door of the new toilets.*

-ch, -tch

There are some simple rules to remind you which form of spelling to use in words that end in a *-ch* when this is pronounced /ch/ as in the word *church*:

• When there is a consonant before it (usually *l*, *n*, or *r*), the spelling is *ch*: *arch, belch, birch, clinch, mulch, perch, search, wrench, zilch.*
• When a double vowel comes before the sound, the spelling is again *ch*: *approach, beach, crouch, debauch, reach, smooch, speech, touch.*

• When a single vowel comes before the sound, the spelling is *tch*: *dispatch*, *ditch*, *fetch*, *notch*, *hutch*.

USAGE NOTE – There are a few important exceptions to the last rule: *attach*, *detach*, *enrich*, *lech*, *much*, *ostrich*, *rich*, *sandwich*, *spinach*, *such*, and *which*. There are also a few words spelt in this way in which the final *-ch* is pronounced /k/ and not /ch/, e.g. *clarsach* (a type of small harp), *Czech*, *distich* (a couplet in poetry), *epoch*, *eunuch*, *loch*, *Sassenach* (a Scottish and Irish name for an English person), *stomach*, and *tech* (short for *technical*). Place names and personal names also have their own rules.

---

changeable

This word meaning 'able to be changed' and also '(of people) fickle, unreliable', is spelt with an *e* in the middle to preserve the soft sound of the *g*.

childish, childlike

Both words are typically used of people who are no longer children. *Childish* is generally unfavourable in tone, suggesting the immature characteristics of children, whereas *childlike* emphasizes the positive and welcome features of childhood, such as innocence and trust:

*Our local councillors are enjoying playing their **childish** party political games while the silent majority of ordinary taxpayers foot the bill.*

*Hyland manages to persuade his audience to join him in a series of exercises which are designed to unlock the joyous **childlike** laughter within us all.*

Childish is sometimes used (wrongly if it implies disapproval when approval is intended) in contexts where *childlike* is needed:

✗ *The first woman might politely be described as pleasant but plain – dark-haired, wearing no make-up and instantly forgettable but for her wildly flapping hands and screams of **childish** [✓ childlike] delight.*

chimney

This has a plural form *chimneys*.

chord, cord

In current usage, there are two words spelt *chord*: a group of notes sounded together in music, and a technical term in mathematics and engineering for a straight line joining two points on the circumference of a circle or joining the front and rear edges of an aerofoil. A *cord* is any of various things that are long and thin, such as a string or rope, an electric wire, a stringlike nerve in the body (especially in *spinal cord*), and (in the plural *cords*) a pair of corduroy trousers (*corduroy* being of uncertain origin but probably connected with the word *cord*).

chronic

See ACUTE, CHRONIC.

claim

When followed by a *that*-clause, *claim* should convey a sense of argument and not mere assertion:

✓ *The dam project has been criticized by conservationists, who* **claim** *that it will ruin the area's rice production.*

✗ *They* **claim** [✓ *allege* or *assert* or *maintain*] *that the animals often suffer from deformities and illnesses.*

When followed by a *to*-infinitive the subject of *claim* should be the same as the subject of the infinitive (so *we claim to be right* is acceptable but *we claim this to be right* is not). This rule forbids a passive construction (as in the second example below):

✓ *Many people* **claim** *to be able to see fairies.*

✗ *A hostile takeover* **is claimed** *to provide a spur for management to strive for greater efficiency.*

classic, classical

Classic means 'of recognized value or merit' or 'serving as a standard of excellence' (*the classic work on the subject, a classic recording*); it is also used as a noun (*the novel has become a classic*), and in the plural *classics* refers to the great literary works of an age, especially those of ancient Greece and Rome. In more general usage, for example when referring to designs or styles, it means 'simple and tasteful' (*a classic kitchen layout*), or simply 'typical and well established' (*the classic symptoms of the disease*).

Classical has special meanings relating to the arts:

the *classical languages* are Greek and Latin, and *classical music* is the music of the eighteenth century before the development of Romanticism (or, more generally, serious mainly European music as distinct from jazz and popular forms of music). *Classical art* and *classical ballet* are the traditional forms as distinct from more modern forms.

clichés and hackneyed words and phrases

A *cliché* is a word or phrase that has become practically meaningless from overuse or overgeneralized use. Notable examples in modern use are *nice, fascinating, meaningful, scenario, viable,* and (more recently) *iconic.* Some are technical terms that are precise in their original meaning but have been adopted in overgeneralized contexts without a real basis of meaning, for example *dimension, interface,* and *parameter.*

HISTORICAL NOTE – *Cliché* is a French word and was originally a term for a photographic negative or printing plate, which produces a cast for printing called a *stereotype* (another word that has spawned a language term). Such words and phrases are also said to be 'hackneyed', a word based on the London place name *Hackney,* where horses were bred for hackney carriages in the days when it was a village. These overworked horses had the special name of *hacks,* and a hackneyed word or expression – like an old hack – is worn out and useless.

Even worse, because their set form makes their unthinking usage that much more obvious, are the hackneyed phrases that riddle bad writing, such as *at this moment in time* and *in this day and age*. Everyone has a mental (or actual) list of phrases that irritate. In their right place they are useful, but too often they are used without any reference to real meaning. Below is a list of those most commonly disliked and best avoided.

to add insult to injury
as a matter of fact
at the end of the day
at this moment in time
the bottom line (is)
the end of the road
to enter a minefield
to explore every avenue
to fall on deaf ears
few and far between
from the bottom of one's heart
in the dim and distant past
in the event that (= if)
in the neighbourhood of (= approximately)
in this day and age
to keep a low profile
last but not least
to lead a dog's life
to leave no stone unturned
a level playing field
the name of the game
to nip in the bud

rotten at the core
six of one and half a dozen of the other
to take on board
until such time as

climactic, climatic

It is easy to confuse these nearly similar words. *Climactic* is a derivative of *climax* and means 'forming or reaching a climax':

*Clive led the British forces at the Battle of Plessey in 1757, one of the **climactic** events leading to the establishment of British rule in India.*

Climatic is based on *climate* and means 'to do with the climate or weather':

*Famines may be caused by **climatic** conditions as well as by pests and diseases.*

coherence, cohesion

Both words come from the verb *cohere* 'to hold together'. *Coherence* is the more abstract in sense, and denotes logical sense and consistency, whereas *cohesion* denotes the physical aspect of sticking together, and might be used about people working together as a team:

✓ *The drama begins to lose **coherence**, with the two most credible characters pushed towards the margins, while the cartoon American monsters occupy centre stage.*

✗ *The biggest risk is lack of* **coherence** [✓ cohesion] *and accountability between organizations.*

✓ *Children centres represent an attempt to put some* **cohesion** *back into communities.*

Cohesion also has a technical meaning of 'molecular attraction' in physics.

The same distinction applies to the corresponding adjectives *coherent* and *cohesive*. *Coherent* broadly means 'making sense' and can be used of a statement or argument or the person making it. *Cohesive* means 'holding together, forming a unit':

Goals were being scored, the defending was solid and players were working as a **cohesive** *unit.*

They can't even put a **coherent** *political statement together outlining their aims and objectives.*

The man called into a police station and reported that he had been car-jacked, though he was barely **coherent**.

colander

See CALENDAR, COLANDER.

collaboration, cooperation, collusion

The three words all relate to one aspect or another of working together. The most positive in meaning is *cooperation*, which implies willing and helpful support. *Collaboration* has sinister undertones because of its political associations of working with an enemy, but it can have more constructive implications. *Collusion*, however, invariably suggests some kind of secrecy or underhand methods or objectives in what is being described:

*Ford's **collaboration** with the Volkswagen Group gave it access to a number of engine and transmission options.*
*As the world becomes more interconnected, the opportunities for global enterprise and **cooperation** grow.*
*They admit to deep frustration in the face of massive government corruption and **collusion** on the part of many police and officials in the drugs trade.*

colleague, comrade

A *comrade* is an active friend or associate, typically a fellow soldier or someone working for a cause that is comparable to a fighting force (such as a radical political movement):

*He died in Afghanistan on Wednesday while trying to save a **comrade** injured in a mine explosion.*
*Most of the signatories to the letter calling on Blair to stand down were linked as old union **comrades** in arms.*

The ordinary word for someone with whom one routinely works from day to day is a *colleague*:

*I'm fascinated by some of my younger **colleagues** and how they seem very much at ease with the technology.*

Using *comrade* in this routine sense, where *colleague* will do, is an affectation to be avoided:

✗ *Many of our **comrades** [✓ colleagues] in the hotel and catering industry work long and unsocial hours.*

collective nouns

This is a name for nouns in English that have a singular form (i.e. they don't end in -*s* or have a plural form like *children*) but refer to several people (usually) or things, for example *audience, committee, crew, family, generation, government, herd, majority,* and *team,* and also less specific words such as *majority* and *proportion*. These nouns can be regarded as singular or plural depending on whether the emphasis is on the members as a group or on the separate individuals that make up the group:

(singular) *We have pre-concert talks but only a small proportion of the audience **is** able to get to those because of the timing.*
(singular) *The government is wasting millions funding a huge array of overlapping adult education agencies.*
(plural) *The crew **were** on schedule with all **their** tasks and **were** not experiencing any problems.*
(plural) *The vast majority of residents **want** to keep the public house, with a smaller number preferring homes to be built on the site.*

The problem only arises with words that have different forms in the singular, i.e. the third person singular present of verbs, and pronouns and determiners such as *its* and *their*. In other types of sentence, the forms of the other words are the same in the singular and plural:

*Their generation **seemed** to think a lot of learning was a good thing.*
*The team **will be** on top form by Saturday.*

The important point to bear in mind is not to mix singular and plural in the same sentence, which can easily be done unthinkingly:

✗ *The British government **is** terrified of offending **their** ally in Washington.*

Here, the verb *is* is singular whereas *their* is plural: we have either to change *their* to *its* or to change *is* to *are* (which works better):

✓ *The British government **is** terrified of offending **its** ally in Washington.*
✓ *The British government **are** terrified of offending **their** ally in Washington.*

When the noun is preceded by a singular determiner such as *a* or *an*, *each* or *every*, or *this*, it has to be treated as singular:

*Each family **has** a chance to comment.*
*This intimate cluster of mop-headed trees not only **provides** a soft umbrella of shade, but also **gives** a sense of privacy.*

But when the collective noun is in the form *a – of* [people or things], it is usually treated as a plural:

*A group of children **were playing** on a see-saw.*
*There **have been** a handful of custody disputes.*

colon *and* semicolon

These two punctuation marks tend to be used less these days in ordinary writing, partly because people are unsure of which to use.

You use a semicolon to link two statements to form a single sentence:

His hair was the mingled colour of rust and cobwebs; his head was bald on top, and the sun beat upon it now.

The semicolon is also useful as a stronger separating mark when there are already commas elsewhere in the sentence:

The explanation, as I shall argue, is likely to be broadly the same for complicated things everywhere in the universe; the same for us, for chimpanzees, worms, oak trees and monsters from outer space.

You use a colon to link two parts of a sentence when the second part expands on or helps to explain the first:

It was on the tip of Alice's tongue to describe the state of the house: cement in the lavatories, loose electric cables, the lot.

The general public has long been divided into two parts: those who think that science can do anything, and those who are afraid that it will.

comic, comical

Comic (as an adjective) is more common than *comical* and is the only one of the two that can be used in the purely descriptive sense 'of or in the nature of comedy' (as in *a comic actor*, *comic roles*, etc.). It also means 'funny, amusing' in a fairly neutral sense with the dramatic or theatrical notion not far away:

*His outspokenness has a natural **comic** mastery the equal of anyone's in this town.*
*The evening had a great variation of works read out, all pieces putting a **comic** slant on everyday life and experiences.*

Comical is more marked in meaning, and tends to convey the notion of absurdity in events or situations:

*Few things are as inherently **comical** as two heterosexual 40-year-old men going on an ice-skating date together.*
*The meal starts at noon and goes on until midnight with talking, drinking, and playing **comical** games.*

comma

Three common errors to avoid involving commas:

• Remember to use a pair of commas to mark a word or phrase that forms an aside or additional reference in a sentence. They have the same role as brackets, but the second comma is often left out:

✗ *Memories, she knew must be painful for him.*
✓ *Memories, she knew, must be painful for him.*
✗ *The President, George W. Bush will address the Assembly.*
✓ *The President, George W. Bush, will address the Assembly.*
✓ *President George W. Bush will address the Assembly.*

(In the last version, *President* is used as a title and the name is added without any commas, not forming an aside.)

• Avoid adding a comma between the subject of a sentence and the continuation, tempting though this is when the sentence is a long one:

✗ *The average income throughout a difficult and at times traumatic year, was less drastically reduced than many had feared.*

• Do not use a comma to join two complete grammatical statements, an error commonly known as the 'comma splice':

✗ *The last six months have just been crazy, we're working until the early hours of the morning.*

If you want to keep the comma, use a linking word such as *and*:

✓ *The last six months have just been crazy, and we're working until the early hours of the morning.*

Alternatively, use a colon or semicolon as explained in the entry above for COLON AND SEMICOLON.

commit

The verb has inflections *commits*, *committed*, *committing*.

common

See MUTUAL, COMMON.

comparable, comparative

Comparable, when used before a noun, implies a definite comparison either with something else or among the things described:

*Super-gentrification began in the mid-1990s and the City workers responsible for it paid £700,000 on average for each terraced house or villa, at least £200,000 more than for **comparable** properties less than a mile away.*

Here, the sense is a little stronger than *similar*, a near synonym that could also have been used in this sentence.

In predicative position (after a verb) it can be followed by *to* or *with*, the choice nominally corresponding to that applying in the case of *compare* (see the separate entry below: *to* likens and *with* contrasts) although, with *comparable*, *to* is much more common and the distinction is less marked:

*Colfer's technological wizardry, Chandler-esque dialogue and comic gusto have built a robust and detailed world, **comparable to** those of J. K. Rowling, Philip Pullman, and Diana Wynne Jones.*

*Mr Clarke's intervention is more **comparable with** those of Michael Heseltine in January 1986 and Norman Lamont in June 1993.*

Comparative is only used before a noun, and the notion, though vaguer, tends to contrast rather than liken. In this use it is an alternative to *relative*:

*The scream of sirens and the drone of helicopters never quite ceased, but there were pockets of **comparative** quiet where people could reflect.*

*The **comparative** cheapness of an operation, plus the favourable exchange rate, means the average cost of a procedure there is half what it would be in the UK.*

The adverb *comparatively* (like *relatively*) is used with the same effect before adjectives and adverbs and other modifying words:

Bisexuality is much more common than is generally believed. ***Comparatively*** *few people have no interest whatsoever in people of their own sex.*
In military terms, most of what the country wants to achieve can probably be accomplished ***comparatively*** *swiftly.*

comparatives *and* superlatives

Adjectives that describe rather than classify (e.g. *cold* and *beautiful,* as distinct from *wooden* and *square*) and adverbs that describe rather than limit or intensify (e.g. *fast* – as in *travel fast* – and *happily,* as distinct from *really* and *only*) have three forms:

- positive (or absolute), e.g. *cold, beautiful, fast*
- comparative, e.g. *colder, more beautiful, faster*
- superlative, e.g. *coldest, most beautiful, fastest*

These forms are used to make comparisons and express extremes (*colder today than yesterday / the coldest day yet / a most beautiful scene / will get there fastest*). Adjectives and adverbs with meanings that allow this kind of comparison are called 'gradable'.

More and *most,* as shown above, are used to form comparative and superlative forms. In addition, gradable adjectives and adverbs of one syllable and some gradable adjectives of two syllables form their comparative and superlative forms by adding *-er* and *-est,* sometimes with a change of the stem (*hard, harder,* *hardest*; *able, abler, ablest*; *common, commoner, commonest*; *happy, happier, happiest*). Adjectives of two syllables ending in *-le* and *-y* usually have these forms: e.g. *nobler, noblest*; *suppler, supplest*; *juicier, juiciest*; *smokier, smokiest*.

Some other two-syllable adjectives also have these forms, but these are less predictable and do not follow a clear rule: the ones in most frequent use are *common, commoner, commonest* and *pleasant, pleasanter, pleasantest*:

*Suicide is a much **commoner** form of death than many people suppose.*

*He had taken the **pleasantest**, south-facing rooms of the house.*

Other adjectives of two syllables, and all adjectives of more than two, normally make their comparative and superlative forms by adding *more* or *most* instead of changing their form (*more honest, more peaceful, most frightening, most remarkable*).

It is important to avoid so-called 'double forms', in which *more* and *most* are attached to adjectives and adverbs that already have the *-er* or *-est* ending, e.g. ✗ *more happier*, ✗ *most fastest*.

compare to, compare with

The difference in usage between *to* and *with* after *compare* causes unnecessary anguish. There is a fairly straightforward rule of thumb: *compare to* likens (remember Shakespeare's *Shall I compare thee to a Summer's day?*) and *compare with* balances and contrasts:

(likening) *Is there anything in life to* **compare to** *that first magic moment: that moment when you realize that there is an infinity of possibilities opening up before you?*

(likening) *A heart is* **compared to** *a seed. Ideas interlink and strange and unexpected connections emerge.*

(likening) *Her publisher* **compared** *her* **to** *'a very frisky golden retriever', adding that she had ignored advice not to do a naked publicity photoshoot.*

(balancing) *There will be a review fee of £250 and possibly an arrangement fee for the new loan. They should* **compare** *this* **with** *other deals, factoring in any fees.*

(balancing) *People were asked to* **compare** *their experiences* **with** *1997, when Labour first won power.*

(balancing) *How much damage could 14-year-old girls do,* **compared with** *fully grown men?*

In the following examples, *to* needs to be replaced by *with*, and vice versa:

✗ *Such private flotations accounted for 22 per cent of the money raised in the European market in the first half of this year,* **compared to** [✓ *with*] *44 per cent over the same period last year.* (The figures are being contrasted, not likened.)

✗ *People are succumbing to this new addiction. It has been* **compared with** [✓ *to*] *crack.* (The addictions are being likened, not contrasted.)

When *compare* is used intransitively (without an object), *with* should be used in BrE because the sense is typically contrastive (although *to* is allowed here in AmE):

*Tally up your own Internet transactions and ask yourself how this **compares with** the turn of the millennium, when going online still felt unnatural to most of us.*

> *For my part, I can compare her to nothing but the Sun; for, like him, she takes no rest, nor ever sets in one place, but to rise in another.*
>
> Colley Cibber, *The Comical Lovers*, 1707

> *In short, the writings of these critics, compared with those of the ancients, are like the works of the sophists compared with those of the old philosophers.*
>
> Joseph Addison in *The Spectator*, 592, 1714

compelling, compulsive

Both words are derived from Latin *compellere* meaning 'to drive on' and share a sense of strong urging. *Compulsive* refers to activities or habits and means 'addictive' or (used of a person) 'addicted':

*One of his **compulsive** gambits was to challenge everyone at the first meeting.*
*I hadn't realized that he was a **compulsive** gambler.*

Compelling is used of arguments and information and means 'convincing' or 'persuasive':

*Haig had one **compelling** argument in favour of attack.*

complacent, complaisant

*We are not **complacent** because we have still got the difficult winter period to come.*

*She responded by striving to ensure that everyone liked her. At school she was a **complaisant** do-gooder, a cheerleader, editor of the school magazine.*

Both words are derived from the Latin verb *complacere* 'to please', and are pronounced the same way apart from the hard -s- sound in the first and the soft -z- sound in the second. *Complacent* typically has un-favourable overtones and means 'calmly or smugly self-satisfied', whereas the much less common word *complaisant* has the more neutral meaning 'inclined to please or comply'. Jane Austen describes Mary Crawford, a character in *Mansfield Park*, as 'complaisant as a sister, . . . careless as a woman and a friend'.

complement, compliment

These two words are frequently confused. A *comple-ment* is something that completes: for example, a *full complement* is the complete crew of a ship or other body of people, and in grammar a *complement* is a part of a sentence that makes the sense complete (as in *They made him **captain***). A *compliment* is an expression of praise or affection (as in *to pay someone a com-pliment*).

The adjectives *complementary* and *complimentary* have corresponding distinctions: something *comple-mentary* serves to complete or enhance, and *comple-mentary colours* produce a neutral colour when combined; a *complimentary remark* is one that praises, and a *complimentary drink* or *ticket* is one given with-out charge, as a kind of compliment.

comply, conform

These words both have to do with acting in accordance with a command or wish or following a piece of advice. *Comply* is typically followed by *with* and *conform* by *to*, and both can be used absolutely, i.e. one can simply *conform* or *comply*, without any grammatical continuation. One *complies* by observing a specific order or instruction, and *conforms* by behaving according to a social convention:

*Michael showed no instinct to **conform**.*
*The whole transaction **conforms** in detail **to** known Hittite law.*
*They obtained an interim injunction against the union, which then agreed to **comply**.*
*All the statutory provisions must be **complied with** before the vehicle can lawfully be driven.*

comprise, compose, consist of, constitute

These words are all used to describe how a whole is made up of its parts, but they look at the situation from different ends. *Comprise* and *consist of* have the whole as the grammatical subject and the parts as the grammatical object:

*The sale **comprises** [or **consists of**] approximately 100 pictures, 100 lots of silver and over 250 pieces of furniture and decorative arts.*
(An alternative is *include*, but this might imply other elements not mentioned.)
*The story line **comprises** a montage of scenes from Henry's life*

intercut with his daughter's quest to learn what happened to her refugee mother.

It is incorrect to use *comprise* the other way round, starting with the parts and leading to the whole:

✗ *100 pictures, 100 lots of silver and over 250 pieces of furniture and decorative arts **comprise** the sale.*

✗ *Nationalist elements **comprised** the major part of the resistance forces.*

In these cases, the verb to use is *constitute* or *compose*:

✓ *100 pictures, 100 lots of silver and over 250 pieces of furniture and decorative arts **constitute** the sale.*

✓ *Nationalist elements **constituted** the major part of the resistance forces.*

✓ *Proteins **compose** much of the actual substance of the human body.*
(You could also use a more general word such as *form* or *make up*.)

It is ungrammatical to use *comprise* in a hybrid passive construction *be comprised of*. Use *consist of* instead:

✗ *We can characterize the human body as a system which **is comprised of** [✓ which consists of or which includes] a number of subsystems.*

✗ *The cargo **was comprised of** [✓ The cargo consisted of] junked vehicles, pipes, tanks, and drilling rig components.*

comrade

See COLLEAGUE, COMRADE.

confidant, confident

The danger here lies in inadvertently misspelling *confident*, an adjective meaning 'sure of oneself, assured about what one does' as *confidant*, turning it into another word, a noun meaning 'a friend to whom one entrusts secrets'.

conform

See COMPLY, CONFORM.

confused words

Words are confused when they are alike in spelling and in some aspect of meaning, as with *appraise / apprise* and *flaunt / flout*. Some pairs are confused in spelling but not meaning (e.g. the verb *forbear* and the noun *forebear*), while in other cases it is the meaning that is the main problem (as with *disinterested* and *uninterested*). In some cases, the confusion is in one direction only, as with *infer*, which overlaps controversially with *imply* although the reverse confusion does not occur. In some cases, the overlap in meaning is considerable enough to make a consistent distinction impossible, as with *sensual* and *sensuous*. Some of the pairs have diverged in meaning over time, having once been much the same (e.g. *continuous* and *continual*; *ensure* and *insure*). In other cases the overlap involves more than two words (e.g. *allusion / illusion / delusion*).

The following are some of the more important sets of words that have separate entries in this book:

adherence	adhesion	
admission	admittance	
adverse	averse	
affect	effect	
all together	altogether	
allusion	illusion	delusion
alternative	alternate	
ambiguous	ambivalent	
amend	emend	
appraise	apprise	
assure	ensure	insure
avert	avoid	evade
baleful	baneful	
biennial	biannual	
blatant	flagrant	
censer	censor	censure
ceremonial	ceremonious	
childish	childlike	
coherence	cohesion	
complacent	complaisant	
complement	compliment	
console	condole	condone
continuous	continual	
council	counsel	
credible	creditable	credulous
currant	current	
decided	decisive	
definite	definitive	
deprecate	depreciate	
discreet	discrete	
disinterested	uninterested	
draft	draught	
eatable	edible	
enormity	enormousness	
especially	specially	

exceptional	exceptionable	
flaunt	flout	
forbear (verb)	forebear (noun)	
forego	forgo	
forever	for ever	
fortunate	fortuitous	
homogeneous	homogenous	
illegal	illicit	
impractical	impracticable	
inapt	inept	
incredible	incredulous	
infer	imply	
ingenious	ingenuous	
interment	internment	
its	it's	
luxuriant	luxurious	
masterful	masterly	
mitigate	militate	
observance	observation	
official	officious	
perquisite	prerequisite	
piteous	pitiable	pitiful
practical	practicable	
precipitate	precipitous	
prescribe	proscribe	
prevaricate	procrastinate	
principal	principle	
purposely	purposefully	
refute	repudiate	
regretful	regrettable	
sensual	sensuous	
slither	sliver	
stationary	stationery	
titillate	titivate	
tortuous	torturous	

consensus

*There is a growing **consensus** at all levels that good universities should be allowed to expand and poor ones shrink or even close in response to student demand.*

The word means 'general agreement' and is spelt -*sensus* and not -*census*. It is related to *consent*, which is a useful way of remembering the correct spelling.

consider

In its meaning 'to regard as being', *consider* can be used in three ways:

• with a simple object followed by a noun or adjective in grammatical agreement with it:

*Rosie is **considered** too old to be moved.*
*People may ignore the dangers or not seek help because they do not **consider** themselves drug users.*

• with a simple object followed by a *to*-infinitive:

*Anyone who **considers** themselves **to be** obese or overweight is welcome to simply drop in to one of the hour-long sessions.*
*There is a stylish restaurant overlooking the garden, **considered to have** one of the best chefs in Garda.*

• followed by *as*, on the analogy of words such as *regard* and *treat*. Unlike the two constructions given above, which are straightforward, this one is more controversial, because *as* is not needed and is therefore arguably redundant (but language often tolerates or even favours redundancy):

? *The figures should be **considered as** a rough approximation.*

Note that *as* is obligatory with *regard*:

✓ *The figures should be **regarded as** a rough approximation.*

console, condole, condone

Console and *condole* overlap slightly in meaning. To *console*, much the more common word, is to comfort someone who is distressed or disadvantaged:

*The England Under 21 star hurled his shirt to the ground and appeared to be close to tears of anger as teammates **consoled** him.*

Console is often used with a reflexive pronoun (*myself, herself, ourselves*, etc.) in the sense 'to take comfort (from some alleviating factor or circumstance)':

*Many of us have **consoled ourselves** with the thought that at least they died happy.*

To *condole* is to sympathize, and is followed by *with*:

*People remain mesmerised by the admixture of sheer evil and staggering woe; at intervals, they issue from their homes to **condole with** one another.*
*She rose up from among the people who had come to **condole with** her on her poor brother's death.*

To *condone* is to pardon or overlook, or even encourage, a wrong act or situation:

*More work has to be done to discourage those parents who **condone** truancy by taking their children out of school for holidays.*

Condole, the least frequent and least familiar of the

three, is the word most often mistakenly used, being confused with *console* or *condone*:

✗ *Next he* **condoles** [✓ *consoles*] *a resident on her cold. 'I felt a bit fluey myself last night.'*
✗ *It's not my role to* **condole** [✓ *condone*] *reckless behaviour.*

contiguous

See ADJACENT, ADJOINING, CONTIGUOUS.

continuous, continual

Continuous means 'continuing without interruption', whereas *continual* means 'recurring repeatedly'. *Continuous* activity goes on all the time without interruption; *continual* activity consists of a series of separate or repeated actions over a period of time:

These countries were involved in effectively **continuous** *diplomatic activity.*
The floor was a **continuous** *mosaic of eight-sided tiles.*
Continual *moaning and criticism of others gets you nowhere.*
Baths were something that caused **continual** *difficulties. There were never enough to go around.*

A synonym for both words is *constant*, which shares both their meanings and is therefore sometimes ambiguous (and hence not a satisfactory alternative): *continual* or *constant* problems are ones that arise from time to time over a period, whereas *continuous* or *constant* difficulty goes on and on without interruption.

Other synonyms are:

- (continual) *recurring, repeated, incessant, perpetual, ceaseless, endless.*
- (continuous) *ceaseless* (again), *endless* (again), *unbroken, unrelieved, steady, persistent, sustained.*

cord

See CHORD, CORD.

correspond to, correspond with

*Leave your answer, name, address, daytime telephone number and the two-digit code that **corresponds to** the venue you would like to attend.*

*Compile a shopping list in which each item **corresponds to** something you know well, maybe rooms of your house.*

*She babbles words that **correspond to** her age.*

In its generic senses *correspond* can normally be used with either *to* or *with*, but note that *with* implies agreement or conformity rather than straightforward similarity or analogy:

*Which painting most **corresponds with** your image of yourself?*

*The Greeting Card Association has issued guidance to members suggesting that they design products to **correspond with** the new postal sizes.*

*The reports we received did not **correspond with** the post-mortem results.*

But in the specific meaning of *correspond* 'to exchange letters', you have to use *with*:

We lost touch with most of the family but his parents still **correspond with** *a few of them.*

coruscate, excoriate

To *excoriate* someone is to criticize them harshly, literally 'to remove their skin', the physical meaning of the word (from Latin *corium* 'skin'):

To his credit, he **excoriated** *the lack of safety at the racetrack.*

To *coruscate* (from Latin *coruscare*) is to glitter or give off flashes of light, and is generally used figuratively:

The next day Minton, in marvellous form and **coruscating** *with wit, took a crowd of friends for a New Year's Day lunch.*

A common error is to use *coruscating* when *excoriating* is intended:

✗ *The government's response is still inadequate, a* **coruscating** *[✓ excoriating] report from MPs warns.*

It might indeed have been better to avoid the trap altogether and use a more straightforward and equally effective word such as *withering* or *blistering* (or, more plainly, *highly critical*). Less troublesome alternatives for *coruscating* include *glittering*, *glowing*, *shimmering*, *dazzling*, and *gleaming*, all words that most readers are likely to understand more readily.

could of

This illiterate adaptation of *could have*, via the contracted form *could've*, is occasionally found in the writing of children and some adults:

✗ You **could of** at least told me.
✗ Things **could of** been a whole lot worse.

Of does sometimes legitimately follow *could*, e.g. when *could* is followed by *of course*:

✓ There **could of course** be other reasons for this.

The incorrect use of *of* for *have* after other modal words such as *might* and *should* is less common, but does occur:

✗ I thought it **might of** been too boring.
✗ You **should of** been at the party last night.

council, counsel

The words are distantly related but their meanings have diverged.

A *council* is a body of administrators, politicians, or academics, or a meeting of them; its members are *councillors*.

Counsel (uncountable, i.e. no plural) is professional advice given by a qualified person, and this person is called a *counsellor*. In Britain, the *Privy Council* is a body of advisers appointed by the monarch, and its members are called *Privy Counsellors*. In America, the spelling is *counselor* and the term also means a court-room lawyer, equivalent to the British *barrister*.

Counsel can also be used as a verb, meaning 'to give advice' and its inflections are *counselled, counselling*:

*I devote a lot of time to **counselling** patients.*

countless

This means 'too many to be counted', and the core meaning is always near the surface. It is too often used indiscriminately as a more colourful synonym for 'very many' or 'numerous'; *innumerable* is a slightly classier alternative that is subject to the same misuse. The result can be counterintuitive or even ridiculous:

? ***Countless** superb composers found their creative lives devastated by this trend towards atonality.*

Superb is a limiting word, and 'superb composers' are by definition a selection based on excellence; and so, quite evidently, they can be readily counted. To call them *countless* is therefore not just an exaggeration but an obvious absurdity.

See also INNUMERABLE.

court-martial

The word for a military court is spelt with a hyphen, both as a noun and as a verb. The plural of the noun is *courts-martial* or *court-martials*, and the verb's inflections are *court-martialled, court-martialling* (although the second of these is rarely needed).

credence, credibility, credit

All three nouns are related in origin and overlap in aspects of their meanings: they are all basically about trust. *Credence* is trust or belief given to a person or, more typically, an idea or proposition, whereas *credibility* is trust or belief received or earned.

*The latest capital spending figures lent **credence** to the view that the Bank of Japan may raise interest rates again by the end of the year.*

*Casual drinkers may give whisky from Wales the same **credence** as they would sherry from Sri Lanka.*

*The energy companies must drop their prices now and end the penalty payments if they are to restore any **credibility** with the public.*

*In a move that will put his **credibility** on the line, the Chancellor gave an upbeat assessment on the state of the negotiations just three months after they collapsed amid bitter acrimony.*

Credit, in its general sense, is acknowledgement or approval given to a person, organization, or action that merits praise:

*The City Council should be given **credit** for recognising that globalisation opens up opportunities as well as threats.*

*Beattie scored after a long absence through injury and won **credit** from his manager for the overall nature of his performance.*

The phrase *to one's credit* is used to recognize praise where it is due, often in the broader context of mixed feelings:

*Forward power was the key factor in the Cornish All Blacks victory, but to their **credit** the Reds gave it their best shot.*

credible, creditable, credulous

Here is a group of adjectives overlapping in core meaning in much the same way as the nouns in the preceding entry.

Credible, the most common of the group, means 'able to be believed, believable' and hence often 'convincing':

*The evidence brought forward was barely **credible**.*
*The Democrats lack a **credible** candidate to be the next President.*

Creditable is a derivative of *credit*, and has to do with deserving praise or acknowledgement:

*Warner finished a **creditable** sixth in the men's event.*
*I would like to offer my congratulations to everyone on their **creditable** achievements.*

Credulous means 'too ready to believe' and is the opposite of *sceptical*:

*Ordinary jurors are thought to be so **credulous** and naive that they cannot be trusted to do as they are instructed by the judge.*

crescendo

In music, a *crescendo* is a passage that gradually increases in intensity and loudness. The common figurative use is based on this notion of gradual ascent, and refers to the process and not the result. Accordingly it should not be used as an alternative for 'peak' or 'climax', which denote a result and not a process:

✗ *The activity reaches a crushing **crescendo**.*
✗ *The onslaught was a shocking **crescendo** to the increased attacks over the past week.*

A more correct use retains the notion of a build-up:

✓ *A **crescendo** of emotion flooded through her.*

criteria

Criteria is a plural noun meaning 'principles by which something is judged'; the singular form, which is less common, is *criterion*:

*Our thinking is still developing and the door is still open for ideas, provided they meet the three key **criteria**.*
*Companies have to meet a series of **criteria** in terms of their commitment to a wide range of issues.*

Like other nouns, such as *data* and *agenda*, because the plural form is much more common than the singular, it has itself taken on the role of a singular noun with a corresponding grammatical construction. But unlike *data*, *agenda*, and other words which have acquired a collective sense in their change from plural to singular, *criteria* clearly refers to several items rather than a group of items and should still be treated as a plural:

✗ *The **criteria** required by the police seems* [✓ *the criteria . . .*
seem or *the criterion . . . seems*] *to keep changing.*

crotch, crutch

Crotch is the part of the human body between the legs
at their junction with the torso; a *crutch* is a support,
either physical (such as a stick used by the infirm), or
figurative (typically political, financial, or emotional):

*He has described the left-wing coalition as a **crutch** for New
Democracy.*
*Her best hope of surviving lies in your willingness to act as a
temporary **crutch** for her.*

Crutch is – confusingly – occasionally found in print
as a variant of *crotch*, but it is best to preserve the
distinction given here.

cruel

The comparative and superlative forms are (in BrE)
crueller, *cruellest*. The American forms are *crueler*,
cruelest.

-ction, -xion

Most nouns with endings of this type are spelt *-ction*:
collection, *deflection*, *distinction*, *extraction*, *protection*,
satisfaction, etc. These are mostly related to words ending in *-ct*, such as *collect* and *deflect*. (*Satisfaction* is
related to *satisfy* via the Latin root *satisfact-*; compare
satisfactory.) In BrE (but not in AmE) a few words of

this type may also be spelt _-xion_: _connexion_, _deflexion_, _genuflexion_, _inflexion_, _reflexion_, _retroflexion_. Finally, there are four words, all based on words already ending in _-x_, that must be spelt _-xion_: _complexion_, _crucifixion_, _fluxion_, and _transfixion_.

For more information on these words, see George Davidson's _Improve Your Spelling_ (in this series), pp. 212–13.

cupful / cupfuls _and related words_

The plural forms of nouns ending in _-ful_ when used as a measure are _cupfuls_, _handfuls_, etc., and not _cupsful_, _handsful_, etc.:

He makes a strong pot of coffee and it does him for the day, warming up the **cupfuls** in a pan as they are needed.
Start adding one piece of fruit or two **handfuls** of vegetables to your dinner every day.
Several **carfuls** of police arrived.

But note the difference between _three cupfuls of water_ (which refers to a measure) and _three cups full of water_ (which refers to actual cups full of actual water). Similarly there is a distinction between _handfuls of glass beads_ and _hands full of glass beads_.

Other words of this type are _earful_, _eyeful_, _forkful_, _spoonful_ (and derivatives such as _tablespoonful_, _teaspoonful_; etc.), and _tankful_.

These should not be confused with adjectives such as _beautiful_, _delightful_, and _skilful_, which obviously do not form plurals.

currant, current

It is easy to confuse these spellings. The first is the dried fruit; the second is a noun meaning 'strong flow' (*carried out to sea by the currents*) and an adjective meaning 'happening or valid now' (*always use the current edition*).

curriculum vitae

The plural is *curricula vitae* (not *vitarum*, although this plural form might also be logical). However, using *CV* (plural *CVs*) is neater and less troublesome.

dangling participles

See PARTICIPLES.

dare, need

These two words are known as 'semi-modal' verbs because they share some of the features of the modal verbs (verbs expressing 'mood') *can*, *could*, *may*, *might*, *must*, *shall* and *will*, and *should* and *would*:

*Her mother **need** never know.* (Compare *Her mother **may** never know.*)
*He doesn't know if he **dare** trust her.* (Compare *He doesn't know if he **can** trust her.*)

Unlike normal verbs, these verbs do not end in *-s* in the third person singular of the present tense (i.e. after *he*, *she*, *it*, or a singular noun) as occurs for example with the verb *end* in the sentence *the story ends in a surprise*. They can also form negatives and questions without the need to use the supporting ('auxiliary') verb *do*:

*I **could not** tell them / I **dared not** tell them.*
***Shall** we stay? / **Need** we stay?*

You cannot say ✗ *the story ends not in a surprise* or ✗ *ends the story in a surprise?* You have to use *do*: ✓ *The story **does not end** in a surprise / ✓ **Does** the story **end** in a surprise?*

Notice that *dare not* and *need not* (and their contracted forms *daren't* and *needn't*) do not use *to* before a following infinitive: ✓ *you need not stay*, not ✗ *you need not to stay* (which could be taken as a slightly stilted way of saying 'you must not stay' i.e. 'you have to leave'). The same applies when *dare* and *need* form questions without *do*: ✓ *dare I say it?*, not ✗ *dare I to say it? How dare you?* is the most common use of *dare* in this sort of question.

USAGE NOTE 1 – *Dare* and *need* also form contracted negative forms *daren't* and *needn't*, on the analogy of *can't, mayn't, mustn't, shouldn't*, etc.:

*He **daren't** tell anyone yet that he had been followed.*

The interesting feature of *dare* and *need* is that, in addition to these modal functions, they can also be used as ordinary verbs conforming to the normal rules of inflection and grammar (this is why they are called *semi*-modals). You can say:

(1) *We **dared not** disagree.*   or
(2) *We **did not dare** to disagree.*
(1) *You **need not** answer yet.*   or
(2) *You **don't need** to answer yet.*

In the type of structure marked (2), it is normal to use *to* after *dare* and *need* (*to disagree, to answer*) although it can sometimes be omitted: *We did not dare disagree* (past tense) is idiomatic but *You don't need answer* (present tense) is awkward.

The choice between these alternative patterns is largely a matter of style and personal preference. The semi-modal patterns tend to be more rhetorical, i.e. they make a stronger point, whereas in their normal behaviour the two verbs are rather more matter-of-fact. But this is not a hard-and-fast rule.

The important point is to avoid mixing the two patterns, for example to use the *dares* form with a direct negative, which is only possible with the *dare* form:

✗ *He only hates because he **dares not** love.*
✓ *He only hates because he **dare not** love.*

USAGE NOTE 2 – Unlike *dare*, *need* in the past tenses is always supported by *do* or *have* to form negatives and questions:

You ***didn't need*** to do that.
Have they needed to borrow money?

*He dare not, for the sake of his own character, refuse
my appeal, even although he were destitute of the
principles of honour and nobleness with which fame
invests him.*

Sir Walter Scott, *Kenilworth*, 1821

data

Data, which means 'information that can be processed', can be either singular or plural. It is plural in
form (from Latin: the singular, which is rarely used, is
datum), and if it is regarded as a collection of pieces
of information it is treated as a plural word, i.e. taking
a plural verb and being used with plural pronouns
such as *these* rather than *this*:

*These **data** show that the largest deforested area is in Central
and South America.*
*Our **data** raise interesting possibilities.*

But *data* is regarded more and more as a 'mass' noun
(rather like the word *news*) denoting a collection of
items to be considered together, and it is therefore
increasingly common to find the word treated as
singular:

*Press a key and be taken directly back to where the **data** was
entered.*
*Missing **data** was not considered in the analysis.*

For much of the time, of course, it is impossible to tell
whether *data* is being used in the singular or plural
because the surrounding words are the same in both
cases:

*You input the **data** only once.*
***Data** can be collected relatively quickly.*
*Their **data** provided little or no support for this notion.*

The important point is not to mix singular and plural in the same context:

✘ *The **data** was collected over several years and once processed provide [✓ provides] some valuable insights.*

dates

When using a numerical notation, bear in mind the differing practice on the two sides of the Atlantic: *3/10/07* (or *03/10/07*) means 3 October 2007 in Britain and 10 March 2007 in North America. The widespread availability of machine-readable forms, in which every box or blank space has to be filled in, has encouraged the general use of zeros to complete single-figure days and months.

decided, decisive

Decided, the past participle of the verb *decide*, is used as an adjective in the senses 'definite or unquestionable' as in *a decided advantage* and 'free of doubt' as in *decided opinions*. It should not be confused with *decisive*, which can refer to events in the sense 'having great importance in deciding the outcome' as in *a decisive battle* and to a person in the sense 'able to make decisions promptly'. Contextualized examples will help to clarify the distinction further:

*Jay liked her eyebrows, straight and black but with a **decided** [= distinct] curve at the end.*

*She felt a **decided** [= definite, unequivocal] unwillingness to open the door.*

*She's a woman of **decided** [= firm, strong] opinions. Won't she want to see me before she takes me on?*

*The world's most famous political prisoner has played a **decisive** negotiating role with the government.*

*A **decisive** victory in battle brought patriotic celebration, while at other times the failure to seek a peace could swing sentiment the other way.*

*The result was widely interpreted as marking a **decisive** shift within the electorate.*

decimate

In current use *decimate* is widely used as a near-synonym for *massacre*, *exterminate*, and similar words. It is used in both physical and figurative contexts:

*A larger French fleet was **decimated** by superior English tactics and the better use of prevailing conditions.*

*Mink are unnecessary killers and have a habit of **decimating** fish stocks if left to breed at the side of fisheries.*

This is practically a reversal of the original meaning, which was 'to kill a selection of (literally, one in ten: see historical note)', and there are language purists who therefore object to the developed meaning the word now has. In time this new meaning will pass unnoticed, but at the moment it remains controversial. It is most acceptable in contexts involving physical death and destruction:

? *Only in AD73, **decimated** by starvation and threatened by the Romans with a large-scale general assault, did the defenders of the citadel commit mass suicide.*

It is much less suited to figurative or abstract meanings that do not involve any physical action:

✗ *Hoteliers who had seen their business **decimated** by the Gulf War were now suffering the ultimate irony of relying on Iraqi visitors to boost their flagging industry.*

✗ *Cuts of that level would **decimate** the existing service.*

HISTORICAL NOTE – The original meaning of *decimate* is 'to kill every tenth person' (usually as a military punishment) and is derived from its use in the context of Roman history: *decimus* is the Latin word for 'tenth'. This meaning has largely died out, along with the practice itself, leaving a useful word with nothing much to do. Usage has therefore given it a new meaning, 'to kill in large numbers' (to reduce *to* a tenth instead of *by* a tenth, perhaps), a practice which is as prevalent as ever.

---

defective, deficient

The two words are both derived from the same Latin word *deficere* 'to desert or fail', and they overlap in meaning, but there is a distinction: the core meaning of *defective* is 'having a fault or defect', i.e. 'not working', while that of *deficient* is 'lacking in some quality or element that is needed', i.e. 'inadequate or insufficient' and can be applied to people, organizations, and things:

*Repointing **defective** mortar is vital to prevent damp in walls.*
*A buyer was entitled to a car, not a running fight with a **defective** machine.*
*This is an unsatisfactory position when what he really wants is to have the **defective** goods repaired or replaced.*

*We tend to be **deficient** in exercise and our muscles tend to become soft and flabby.*
*There is something sad about grown men waving guns about like that. It makes me wonder if they aren't **deficient** in some other aspect of their lives.*
*Each department submitted a list of topics and noted those in which library resources were **deficient**.*

definite, definitive

Definite has the more self-contained meaning 'clear of all ambiguity or doubt':

*Having a climbing partner who was fluent in French, English, Spanish, and Catalan, was a **definite** [= distinct, clear] advantage.*
*She has **definite** [= firm, decided] ideas on how she thinks things should be organized.*
*The recession shows **definite** [= clear, unmistakable] signs of coming to an end.*
*It is important for the project to have a **definite** [= clearly defined and limited] goal.*

Whereas *definitive* looks more to consequences in its meaning 'providing the required outcome or authority':

*Such is the variety of expression that people use that no **definitive** [= conclusive, exhaustive] grammar of English exists.*
*The joint committee's objective was to propose a **definitive** [= categorical, conclusive] standard of accounting and financial reporting.*
*Of the contenders lining up to replace me it's hard to give a **definitive** [= authoritative, conclusive] verdict.*

defuse, diffuse

Defuse is a verb with the literal meaning 'to remove a fuse from (a bomb)'. It is commonly used in a figurative sense 'to reduce the tension in (a difficult situation)':

*A jobs package will go some way to **defusing** criticism over a perceived lack of direction in tackling the dole queues.*
*Whenever the tension mounted, he **defused** it with a razor-edged comment.*

Diffuse is a verb meaning 'to spread over a wide area' and also an adjective in the corresponding sense 'widely spread'. It has a wide range of applications, of which the following examples are typical:

*As managers become more confident that **diffuses** through the rest of the organization, so staff become more confident too.*
*The attempt to meet this **diffuse** and stateless threat primarily with weapons and concepts devised for interstate warfare has been a costly error.*

It is a common mistake, especially in newspaper reports, to write *diffuse* for *defuse*:

✗ *Our strategy must also include an effort to* **diffuse** [✓ *defuse*] *the hatred and misunderstanding in the Muslim world that fuels al-Qaeda.*

delusion

See ALLUSION, REFERENCE, ILLUSION, DELUSION.

dependant, dependent

It is easy to choose the wrong spelling, as the core meanings are the same and it is the grammar that differs. The first is a noun, and the second is an adjective.

A *dependant* is a person who depends on another for support financially and in other ways:

An increasing number of ex-service personnel and their **dependants** *are now reaching the age where they need some form of supportive housing.*

Dependent is typically followed by *on* and means 'relying on someone or something for support':

Samoa is not overly **dependent** *on tourism and has little in the way of luxury hotels.*

Dependent on also means 'having as a necessary condition':

The immediate future of the agency is partly **dependent on** *a favourable recommendation in the imminent report.*

deprecate, depreciate

The two words overlap, but only slightly, in senses to do with disapproval. The main meaning of *depreciate* is 'to decline in value' as applied for example to money or other assets:

*People want to save in a currency that does not **depreciate** every year.*

In this sense *deprecate* plays no role, but *depreciate* can also signify undervaluing in the more abstract sense of belittling or disparaging:

*Was Angus actually mocking Paine, his chosen prophet, or merely **depreciating** himself?*
*She seems to **depreciate** nature itself as if her whistling were better and more melodious than birdsong.*

Deprecate, from Latin *deprecari* 'to avert by prayer' (from *precari* 'to pray'), has a similar meaning 'to deplore' but implies disapproval or scorn rather than belittling:

*We utterly **deprecate** the imposition by Westminster of alien moral standards upon Ulster.*
*He sniffed in a **deprecating** way and eyed Charles's uniform.*

derisive, derisory

The two words are both derived from the Latin word *ridere* 'to laugh': *derisive* is active in sense and means 'scornful [as though laughing]', whereas *derisory* is passive in its sense 'fit to be laughed at', i.e. 'absurdly or ludicrously inadequate', used typically in the context of sums of money, offers, etc.:

*With a **derisive** snort, she turned away to make the tea.*
*His tone was openly **derisive**.*

*The workers feel the offer is **derisory**.*
*It was sold at auction for a **derisory** sum by Josef II in 1782.*

The more common error is to use *derisory* when *derisive* is needed:

✗ *She gave a short, **derisory** [✓ derisive or mocking] laugh.*

despite, in spite of

These two prepositions are largely interchangeable and both can be followed by nouns or noun phrases or by constructions introduced by a participle (a verb ending in *-ing*):

***Despite** initial scepticism, the deal is poised to go ahead.*
*He managed to shoot down 33 fighter-bombers, **despite** being grounded for 10 days.*
***In spite of** all the problems, it is worth the effort.*

In all these examples, *despite* could be replaced by *in spite of* and vice versa.

If a clause with a verb has to follow, this must be linked with *the fact that* and not simply *that*:

*He still looks young, **despite** [or in spite of] the fact that he's a grandfather.*

> USAGE NOTE – *Although* or *even though* can often replace the unwieldy sequence 'despite the fact that' without any loss of meaning:
>
> *He still looks young **even though** he's a grandfather.*

different from / to / than

The adjective *different* is typically used with three linking words: *from*, *to*, and *than*. Of these, the safest choice in BrE – because it is the only one that everyone accepts – is *from*:

*Those closest to him describe a man who is very **different from** his public image.*
*I fell for Calum because he was **different from** any boyfriend I've had.*
*Styling is quite **different from** what you'd actually choose in real life.*
*Nearly everything he did was very public-spirited and very **different from** the kinds of things I get up to.*

The preference for *from* is based on the argument that because we say that one thing *differs from* another, we should say that one thing is *different from* another. But English is not always as logical as this. For example, we say *accord with* but *according to*. In actual use, as distinct from the theory, *different* is followed by *to* as well as *from*:

*Preparations were vastly **different to** his first attempt in the 1960s.*

In AmE, *than* is much more common, especially when a clause containing a verb follows:

*The way you were treated by the teachers if you were staying on was a lot **different than** if you were leaving.*

In BrE it is often preferable to rephrase, since the construction with *than* jars with some readers:

✓ *The way you were treated by the teachers if you were staying on **differed** a lot **from** the way they treated you if you were leaving.*

In some sentences, especially when *different* is separated from the continuation it relates to, *from* can sound inelegant; in these cases *to* or even *than* is more natural:

✓ *It's a very **different** country **to** the one in which he grew up.*
✓ *This is clearly one of those words that means something **different** in French **to** English.*
✓ *A false sense of security which makes drivers behave quite **differently** on motorways **than** on ordinary roads.*

HISTORICAL NOTE – Objection to *different to* is fairly recent. Several well-known writers of nineteenth-century fiction preferred it, for example:

He never thinks of you. – Such fickleness! Oh! how different to your brother and to mine! I really believe John has the most constant heart.

Jane Austen, *Northanger Abbey*, 1818

> *Something in my mind whispered to me that the smear on your nightgown might have a meaning entirely different to the meaning which I had given to it up to that time.*
>
> Wilkie Collins, *The Moonstone*, 1868

diffuse

See DEFUSE, DIFFUSE.

dilemma

A *dilemma* is a choice between two alternatives neither of which is conclusively satisfactory. It is not simply a synonym for 'difficulty' or 'difficult choice'. The following example is somewhat longer than usual, so as to provide more context to reinforce the meaning:

*In private, he became ever more tormented by the fact that his research work on pancreatic cancer was leading to drugs being tested on animals. Faced with an increasing moral **dilemma** and the estrangement of his girlfriend, who despised animal testing, he turned to violent activism to help ease his conscience and at the same time please her.*

Dilemmas typically involve choices based on conflicting morals or principles, as in the example just given, and so you will often find the term *moral dilemma* used.

The notion is well characterized by the phrase *on the*

horns of a dilemma, meaning 'faced with two equally unwelcome alternatives'. Horns tend to come in pairs, and by avoiding one of the horns one runs the risk of being caught on the other. There is always this duality contained in the idea of a dilemma.

In the following example, the choices are unexpressed or undefined, so that the use of *dilemma* is questionable:

? *A beggar recognizes him in the street, catapulting him into the **dilemma** [✓ choice or problem] of how much money to give him.*

In the next example, there is a better alternative to *dilemma*:

? *She faces the perennial **dilemma** [✓ conflict] between touring and the need to fulfil family commitments.*

As a guiding rule, if in place of *dilemma* you can substitute words such as *choice*, *decision*, *difficulty*, or any of those given above without affecting the meaning, it is better to use them.

discreet, discrete

These two words are related in origin, are pronounced the same way, and are often confused. Their meanings are different.

Discreet means 'careful to avoid giving offence or betraying a confidence' and can refer to a person or an action:

*Bodie stopped the car at a **discreet** distance from the blue van.*

*He didn't want the Russians getting to him, so he had to be very **discreet.***

Discrete means 'separate or distinct':

*Justice and politics are never **discrete** entities.*

discriminating, discriminatory

Both words are based on the noun *discrimination* in two different senses. *Discriminating*, when used as an adjective, means 'showing good taste or judgement' and has favourable overtones (*caters for discriminating customers*), whereas *discriminatory* means 'showing discrimination or prejudice' and is unfavourable (as in *discriminatory behaviour, policies, practices*, etc.).

disinterested, uninterested

In current English, *disinterested* does not mean the same as *uninterested*; it has a meaning that is quite distinct, relating as it does to a different sense of the root word *interest*. To express the meaning 'not interested' in the core sense 'not wanting to know about or be involved in something', the word to use is *uninterested*:

*An animal behaviourist at Manchester University has found that mice are totally **uninterested** in cheese.*
*I was mistrustful, initially, that a long poem could hold my attention, let alone that of an **uninterested** schoolchild.*

Disinterested means 'not having an interest', but the sense of interest involved here is 'personal concern or advantage', i.e. *disinterested* means 'impartial':

*So many believe the church to be totally **disinterested**. I am striving to show that the church can be relevant, and have a positive influence.*

*The diplomatic service proffers sage and **disinterested** advice to ministers.*

*A **disinterested** third party was brought in to help to broker an agreement between the clubs.*

Despite the best efforts of many, *disinterested* has more recently and controversially begun to revert to its older meaning, coinciding with *uninterested* and sharing the preposition *in* as its link word:

✗ *Service does not always come with a smile, as anyone who has had a meal thrust in front of them with a scowl or been greeted by **disinterested** [✓ uninterested or apathetic] staff will testify.*

✗ *Spendaholic women blow more than they earn on fashion and are **disinterested** in [✓ uninterested in or unconcerned about] homes, jobs, and careers, a survey has revealed.*

The special meaning of *disinterested* is certainly worth preserving, and since in most cases, including the sentences given above, the more straightforward word *uninterested* can be substituted, this is the best course.

HISTORICAL NOTE – This issue is a perfect example of how problems of usage can lie in the history of words. Both words used to have the same meaning, which is that corresponding to *uninterested* in modern use, i.e. 'lacking interest' in the main sense of *interest*. But in the seventeenth century *disinterested* acquired a new meaning 'impartial, unbiased', and this stems from another meaning of *interest*, 'personal advantage or involvement'. The old meaning of *disinterested* disappeared, and *uninterested* was left to cope with it, establishing a distinction between two closely related words. This state of affairs continues in modern use, and is vigorously defended by those who do not want to see a useful distinction become eroded, even though there are alternative words such as *unbiased, detached, indifferent*, and above all *impartial*. (There is also *unconcerned*, but this too can involve ambiguity as it has variations of meaning corresponding to those of its root word *concern*.)

There is no Conduct so fair and disinterested, but that it may be misunderstood by Ignorance, and misrepresented by Malice.

Henry Fielding, *Tom Jones*, 1749

dissatisfied, unsatisfied

The usual word, in the marked sense 'disappointed' or 'unhappy', is *dissatisfied*:

*He had become **dissatisfied** [= disappointed, discontented] as a draughtsman and chose to redirect his talents to story-telling.*
*With a last **dissatisfied** [= discontented, displeased] glance in the mirror, she left the bedroom and made her way downstairs.*

Unsatisfied is a useful alternative, free of the emotional overtones of *dissatisfied*, when the meaning is more neutrally 'not (yet) satisfied':

*One of my few remaining **unsatisfied** [= still to be satisfied] ambitions is to get into the old man's study.*
*The compromise left all sides **unsatisfied** [= not satisfied, unwilling to agree].*

dissent, dissension

The two words have a common origin in the Latin word *sentire* 'to feel' (with the prefix *dis-* denoting lack or deprivation). *Dissent* involves disagreement with or rejection of an opinion or policy:

*The howl of **dissent** that came from the entire room staggered me.*
*To permit **dissent** within the Party would be to reopen the door to bourgeois deviations.*

Whereas *dissension*, while also denoting disagreement, implies strong discord:

*The club was the victim of **dissension** at the top which permeated down to the players.*
*Until 1939 internal **dissension** remained characteristic of the Labour Party.*

distinct, distinctive

The core meaning of *distinct* is 'definite or clearly perceptible':

*There was a **distinct** possibility that companies would use mass lay-offs.*
*There was a **distinct** lingering odour of tobacco and dogs.*

It also carries the notion of separateness from something or someone comparable, and in this use may be complemented by *from*:

*Being young affects attitudes to breaking the law in two **distinct** ways.*
*This sort of dream seems **distinct from** any recollections of flying in an aeroplane.*

Distinctive means 'characteristic' and implies typicality rather than just clarity:

*He weighs 10 lbs and wears **distinctive** red booties.*
*There was a **distinctive** runway mown in the centre of the course.*
*He had a **distinctive** hooked gold earring in his left ear.*

do

Do is a convenient catch-all verb that can stand in for other verbs, and for verb-based phrases, to avoid having to repeat them:

*No one makes scones like his mother **does** [makes scones].*
*The students could not understand what he was saying, although his colleagues always **did** [understood him].*

*We're not supposed to use the photocopier, but we **do** [use the photocopier].*
*Will you come with us, like you used to **do** [come with us]?*

The words in square brackets, which are not of course actually used, supply what is implied by the presence of the verb *do*.

As with many useful devices in language, there are traps for the unwary. In particular, beware of using *do* in this way when it does not fit the grammar:

✗ *She is earning more money than her sisters **do**.*

The final *do* in this sentence does not fit with the previous verb, which already has the auxiliary verb *is*, and so *are* is needed instead:

✓ *She is earning more money than her sisters are.*
   (Or simply, ✓ *She is earning more money than her sisters.*)

double subject

If you have a sentence with a double subject joined by *and*, take care to use a plural verb. In longer sentences, when a subject of this type is separated from its verb by other words, the grammar can become confused, especially when the words joined by *and* seem to form a unit:

✗ *The assessors came to the conclusion that the approach and method used in the experiment was [✓ were] flawed.*

doubtful, dubious

Doubtful and *dubious* are interchangeable in the meanings 'causing doubt' and 'uncertain', although *doubtful* tends to be preferred when referring to a person and *dubious* when referring to an idea or concept:

*Which of the **dubious** / **doubtful** benefits of civilization would you introduce them to next, I wonder.*
*I am **doubtful** / **dubious** about the wisdom of making endless repairs to these very old boats.*

In the meaning 'expressing doubt', when applied to looks, gestures, responses, and so on, *doubtful* and not *dubious* should be used:

*A **doubtful** look crossed his face.*

Doubtful can be followed by *that* or *whether*, whereas *dubious* cannot:

*We are **doubtful** whether this idea will work.*

And in the meaning 'open to question, of questionable value or worth', *dubious* and not *doubtful* is the choice:

*The appeal was rejected on **dubious** grounds.*

doubt if / whether / that

When *doubt* is used to mean 'to think something unlikely', the standard way of linking it with what follows (the object of the doubt) is with *if* or *whether*, and the same applies when *doubt* is a noun in phrases such as *there is doubt*:

*I **doubt if** I could have resisted the temptation.*
*I **doubt if** it ever dawned on him that his patient wife might tell him to get stuffed.*
*There was some **doubt whether** another child had pushed him or not.*
*He **doubts whether** some countries will be able to clamp down on smuggling.*

But when *doubt* is used negatively (with *no*, *not*, etc.) to express in effect likelihood rather than its opposite, the link word is normally *that*:

*There is little **doubt that** there is some truth in the story.*
*There is no reason to **doubt that** the money will be made available at this stage.*
*He had no **doubts that** the parents in this case were innocent.*

As usual, the *that* of the *that*-clause can be omitted informally:

*No one **doubts** eating five bars of chocolate for lunch is unhealthy eating.*
*I don't **doubt** there was something really wrong.*

HISTORICAL NOTE – This distinction is supported by the logic of what is involved in doubting. When *doubt* is grammatically positive its meaning suggests uncertainty in the following clause (for which *if* and *whether* are more suitable) whereas not doubting, which is grammatically negative, has a positive result, making a *that*-clause more logical.

Many people dislike the increasing use of a *that*-clause (or a clause with *that* omitted) after a use of *doubt* in the affirmative:

? *I **doubt that** she'll do it before she's finished her exams.*
? *The Prime Minister returned amid growing **doubts that** the treaty would ever become law in its present form.*
? *He **doubted** it would make any difference.*

This usage is widely regarded as an Americanism, but it is found in British English from the end of the nineteenth century and is now common. Nonetheless, it remains controversial.

downward, downwards

See BACKWARD, BACKWARDS, *AND RELATED WORDS*.

draft, draught

Draft is the spelling in BrE for the noun meaning 'a preliminary version of a piece of writing' and the corresponding verb meaning to write one (*will draft an amendment*). It is also used in the banking sense and in senses to do with recruitment (although in military contexts *conscription* is more usual; *draft* is AmE). *Draught* is a noun and is used in senses to do with movement of air, depth of water, and amounts of liquid (especially alcohol). In AmE *draft* tends to be preferred for all these meanings.

dubious

See DOUBTFUL, DUBIOUS.

due to

Pentonville's overcrowding was **due to** *a rise in remanded and unsentenced prisoners.*
Statistics show an increasing trend in reported incidents. We believe **this** *is mainly* **due to** *a greater understanding that domestic abuse is unacceptable.*

This apparently simple little phrase causes a great deal of trouble. Since *due* is an adjective it works best when there is a specific antecedent noun or noun phrase it can refer to. In each of the sentences given above, *due to* has an antecedent shown in bold.

   There is, on the other hand, much disapproval of the use of *due to* when it lacks a clear noun or pronoun antecedent:

? *The company warned results for the current financial year would not be as strong* **due to** *transition to a new product range.*

? *Sinclair Court is a property that lends itself to this type of development* **due to** *its flat roof and overall design.*

In these sentences, a linking phrase such as 'and this is/was' or 'and this fact is/was' is needed before *due to* to provide an antecedent and make the grammar work satisfactorily:

✓ *The company warned results for the current financial year* *would not be as strong, **and this was due to** transition to a new product range.*

✓ *Sinclair Court is a property that lends itself to this type of development, **and this fact is due to** its flat roof and overall design.*

An alternative strategy that avoids this kind of grammatical manipulation is to use *because of* or *owing to*, which are structurally freer of the preceding part of the sentence:

✓ *The company warned results for the current financial year would not be as strong, **because of** transition to a new product range.*

✓ *Sinclair Court is a property that lends itself to this type of development, **owing to** its flat roof and overall design.*

Note also that *due* and *to* can come together with a different meaning, when *due* means 'required or expected' and *to* is linked to a following infinitive. In this case *due* always qualifies a preceding noun or pronoun:

*The youth is **due to** be sentenced at the Old Bailey in March.*

each, every

Both words denote all the people or things in a group, and both normally take a singular verb, but the meaning differs in that *each* regards the people or things concerned separately, whereas *every* regards them collectively. There are some other important differences in usage:

• *each* is a pronoun and can stand on its own (*there are six of each / each of the houses has a garden*) as well as a determiner (*there are six of each kind*), whereas *every* is only a determiner (✓ *there are six of every kind /* ✓ *every one of the houses has a garden*).

• *each* can refer to two or more items, whereas *every* typically refers to three or more.

Singular or plural?

Each is treated as singular when it stands by itself as a pronoun, when it comes before a singular noun (*each house*), and when it is followed by *of* and a plural noun (*each of the houses*):

Each case has to be examined on its merits.
I will try to give a summary of what each of the theories attempts to explain.

When *each* follows and qualifies a plural noun or pronoun, it is treated as a plural since it is the noun or pronoun and not *each* that determines the singular or plural status of the sentence:

They each carry scars left by the trauma of war.
The courses each consist of a series of modules.

Every is used with a singular noun and is always followed by a singular verb:

Every adult has to contribute something to the upkeep of the neighbourhood.
Every day was like a hurdle in a steeplechase for her.
He knew that every problem has a solution.

Avoid *each and every*, which is a stylistically poor cliché:

? *He had seen to it that each and every boy found his way into a suitable occupation.*

If you want to emphasize individuality in this way use *each* or *every single*.

each other, one another

The view that *each other* refers to two people or things and *one another* to more than two is a superstition long ago rejected or ignored by good writers (see the contrary examples below). Modern usage sensibly follows:

*Banks are always lending money to **each other**.*
*Jane and I could only see **one another** at weekends.*

In each of these examples, *one another* could be substituted for *each other* and vice versa with no effect on the meaning.

When used alongside *both*, however, *each other* is more natural:

*I think we're **both** as annoying as **each other**.*

> *You and Mr. Elton are by situation called together; you belong to one another by every circumstance of your respective homes.*
>
> Jane Austen, *Emma*, 1815

> *I have endeavoured in this ghostly little book, to raise the ghost of an idea, which shall not put my readers out*

*of humour with themselves, with each other, with the
season, or with me.*

Charles Dickens, Preface to *A Christmas Carol*, 1843

Note that *each other* is reflexive in use, i.e. it refers
back to a grammatical subject earlier in the sentence (*Banks*, and *Jane and I*, in the examples given
above). It should not itself be used as the subject of a
verb:

✗ *They read every email **each other** sends.*
✓ *They **each** read every email **the other** sends.*

eatable, edible

Eatable means 'fit for eating' in the sense 'pleasant to
eat' and tends to be used in negative contexts (*the meal
was barely eatable*). *Edible* also means 'fit for eating'
but in the sense of being inherently suitable and not
poisonous (*not all mushrooms are edible*).

economic, economical

Pairs of adjectives ending in *-ic* and *-ical* tend to have
slightly different meanings and are not always interchangeable: others are *classic/classical*, *comic/comical*,
and *historic/historical*. For some reason the pair *econ-
omic/economical* seems to cause more problems than
most.

As is usual with words of this type, the form in *-ic*
is the basic one meaning 'to do with economics' or 'in
terms of the economy' (in its sense 'the structure of
financial organization in a country'):

*A low level of unemployment should be the guiding principle of a government's **economic** policy.*
*The issue is a simple one of **economic** competence.*

It can also mean 'efficient and profitable':

*Tufted carpets are much more **economic** to produce.*
*A report questioned whether the export prices would be **economic** if all costs were included.*

The form in *-ical* tends to mean 'providing or practising economy' (in the sense 'value for money') with 'economy' being interpreted fairly broadly (e.g. economy of movement as well as financial economy, and economy of honesty in the catchphrase *economical with the truth*):

*The hotel is conveniently near the station with rooms at **economical** prices.*
*His music is far more **economical** in melody and orchestral sound.*

You can often see the difference in meaning if you substitute one word for the other in the same sentence:

*We need to find more **economic** [= profitable] forms of foreign travel.*
*We need to find more **economical** [= inexpensive] forms of foreign travel.*

edible

See EATABLE, EDIBLE.

edgy

The traditional meaning of edgy is 'peevish and irritable' and is derived from the idiom *one's nerves are on edge*. There is however a recent new meaning 'at the forefront of ideas, trendy', which is based on another idiom, *at the cutting edge*:

A former fashion director of Style *magazine, she was revered for her **edgy** enthusiasm and originality.*

It is as well to be aware of the potential ambiguity caused by this development in meaning.

effect

See AFFECT, EFFECT.

effective, effectual, efficacious, efficient

All these words mean 'having a good or desired effect' of one kind or another, but with different connotations and shades of meaning, which also apply to the corresponding adverbs *effectively*, *effectually*, *efficaciously*, and *efficiently*.

Effective denotes an effect that is actual rather than theoretical:

*Will antivirus software be **effective** for much longer?*
*Sir Christopher's success has been rooted in understanding what it is to be an **effective** chairman.*
*The measures have been **effective** in helping prevent further outbreaks.*

Effectual means 'capable of producing the required result or effect', regardless of personal involvement, and tends to be theoretical rather than actual:

*Further legislation was deemed necessary 'for the more **effectual** Suppression of the Slave Trade'.*
*The eleven-plus **effectually** brands the majority of children as failures before they are mature enough to make decisions.*

Effectual is not typically used to describe a person, but *ineffectual* is, with the meaning 'lacking the ability to produce results':

*The father, an **ineffectual** university academic, has moved out and seems disinclined to offer any help.*

Efficacious applies only to things, and means 'proven or sure to produce the required effect'. It refers typically to treatments, solutions, courses of action, and the like:

*Similar work can be done in rehabilitation centres to encourage and reward those treatments that prove **efficacious**.*
*Holidays are supposedly good for you and this one has been notably **efficacious**.*

Efficient refers to a person's or thing's capacity to produce results with the least effort and at the least expense:

*County bosses say savings made will be ploughed back into children's services and insist the move will make the service more **efficient**.*
*We have one of the most **efficient** financial systems in the world.*

*The coach drivers are always very **efficient**, courteous, and friendly.*

Note also that *efficient* has come to be used in hyphenated combination with words for resources to denote effective use of that resource, e.g. *cost-efficient, energy-efficient,* and *fuel-efficient.*

-ei- *or* -ie-

See -IE- *OR* -EI-.

either, neither

These words are flexible in their grammatical roles and can be used as adjectives (or more accurately, determiners: *either one / neither option*), pronouns (*either of them / took neither*), and conjunctions (*either it is or it isn't*). *Either,* but not *neither,* is also an adverb (*that's not true either*).

As an adjective or pronoun, *either* and *neither* should refer to two people or things and not several:

*This crucial point in their relationship had not come too soon for **either** of them.*

If the reference is to more than two, use *any* instead of *either* and *none* instead of *neither.*

When *either* or *neither* is the subject of a verb, the verb is typically put in the singular, although *neither* can idiomatically also take a plural verb when the sense calls for it:

Either of the proposed solutions is adequate for our immediate purpose.
Neither of these claims is self-evident as it stands. (Emphasis is on each.)
*The wonder is that **neither** of them ever put on much weight.* (Emphasis is on both.)

When used to show pairs of alternatives, *either* is balanced by *or* and *neither* is balanced by *nor*:

*The scale of the problem has not been assessed **either** nationally **or** locally.*
*The internees **either** remained in Australia for vital war work **or** joined the labour units of the Australian army.*
*Neither a first-rate performance of a symphony **nor** a miserable one will change what the composer wrote.*
*You should **neither** smoke **nor** drink alcohol in a state of shock as this further affects the blood pressure.*

Again the reference should be to two alternatives and not several (a further alternative can be added on as shown in the second example below, preserving the correct balance for the *either . . . or . . .* grouping):

✗ *The problem can be **either** resolved, referred upwards, **or** shelved.*
✓ *The problem can be **either** resolved **or** referred upwards, **or** it can be shelved.*

USAGE NOTE – Take care to balance the two halves of an *either . . . or . . .* and *neither . . . nor . . .* sentence correctly:

✓ *Hathor is depicted **either** as a beautiful young woman **or** as a rather sad cow.*

✓ *Hathor is depicted as **either** a beautiful young woman **or** a rather sad cow.*

✗ *Hathor is depicted **either** as a beautiful young woman **or** a rather sad cow.*

✗ *Hathor is **either** depicted as a beautiful young woman **or** as a rather sad cow.*

The last two versions are poorly formed because the two sides of the *either . . . or . . .* structure do not match. You can always test this by comparing what follows *either* with what follows *or*. In the last sentence, *either* is followed by the verb *depicted*, whereas *or* is followed by the complement *as a rather sad cow* without any verb present. In the first, *either* and *or* are both followed by balancing statements (*as a beautiful woman* and *as a rather sad cow*), and in the second the balance is achieved by the corresponding noun phrases *a beautiful young woman* and *a rather sad cow*.

When the two alternatives share the same number (i.e. are both singular or both plural) in a sentence of the following type, they are collectively treated as singular or plural correspondingly:

Either he **or** the bird **is** going to have to go.

Neither Palestinians from East Jerusalem *nor* overt supporters of the Palestine Liberation Organization *were* to be allowed to attend the conference.

A problem arises when one of the alternatives in an *either . . . or . . .* or *neither . . . nor* construction is singular and the other plural. In these cases, the rule is to make the verb agree with the one closer to it:

✓ *Either* the architect *or* the builders have to specify the plant and scaffolding needed.
✓ He'll make sure *neither* the wife *nor* the two boys ever want for anything.
✓ *Neither* the market *nor* the media like to be taken by surprise.

But it is often better to recast the sentence entirely, as with the first and third of these examples:

✓ *Either* the architect has to specify the plant and scaffolding needed *or* the builders have to.
✓ The market does not like to be taken by surprise, *nor* do the media.

emend

See AMEND, EMEND.

emotional, emotive

Both words mean 'connected with or appealing to the emotions': *emotional* is more often used in the neutral sense 'relating to or involving emotion' whereas *emotive* conveys stronger notions of 'causing emotion':

They benefit from parenting help, practical and **emotional** *support and leisure activities.*
The woman gave an **emotional** *press conference at which she said her house would seem empty without her daughter there.*
It was very **emotional** *winning the gold at the World Rowing Championships.*

Emotional also means 'easily affected by emotion' with reference to people, a meaning that *emotive* lacks:

An **emotional** *Kershaw told how his world had collapsed.*

Emotive describes behaviour or language that might arouse emotions and tends to be disapproving, whereas *emotional* describes feeling and actions that involve emotion in themselves and is more positive in tone:

It was a reasonable debate on an issue which is all too often the subject of **emotive** *soundbites.*
The family of a young father taken hostage in Iraq have issued an **emotional** *appeal for his release.*

It will be clear that there is a considerable overlap in meaning between these two words, as is shown by the fact that the two words can be exchanged in many of the examples without causing any major difference to their basic meaning. However, the connotations and undertones are often different.

enormity, enormousness

Enormity has a special meaning that is usefully preserved. It means properly 'great wickedness', 'dreadful scale', or 'a wicked or terrible' act, and it is wasted as a substitute for *enormousness* in the plain sense 'great size':

✓ *It took a while for the full **enormity** of what was happening to filter through.*

✓ *The **enormities** of the Stalin era are the subject of a new historical study.*

✗ *There are times when the **enormity** of the city overwhelms you.*

✗ *Despite the **enormity** of these changes, much of the nineteenth-century conception remained.*

Unfortunately the alternative *enormousness* is ungainly in speech, and this may be why the much neater word *enormity* is forcing it out, but there are other alternatives that get round the problem, such as *hugeness, immensity, magnitude,* or *vastness,* or phrases such as *huge* (or *great*) *size, far-reaching nature,* or *vast scale* (or *proportions*). Alternatively, the sentence can be recast more drastically, for example:

✓ *Although these changes were far-reaching, much of the nineteenth-century conception remained.*

ensure

See ASSURE, ENSURE, INSURE.

equable, equitable

Both words are derived from the Latin word *aequus* meaning 'equal', but their meanings are different.

Equable means 'even and moderate, regular' and typically describes major forces in nature, such as climate, personality, and temperament. It denotes avoidance of extremes as well as avoidance of change:

*His social conscience had always been strong, even if his nature was too **equable** to be consumed by horror and disgust at the human condition.*

Equitable means 'just, fair' (usually when there are several parties involved). It is typically used with words to do with agreement, principle, and resolution:

*It would be perfectly possible to move towards a more **equitable** tax system and maintain revenue.*

-er, -or

Take care not to misspell words that end in *-er* and *-or*.

- *-er* is freely used to form nouns for people and things that carry out some activity (*adviser, baker, builder, mixer, opener, usurper, worker*).
- *-er* is also used in a few words that are not derived from verbs and mostly denote people (*foreigner, jeweller, lawyer, mariner, prisoner, sorcerer, treasurer, usurer*).
- *-or* is used in the following words:

accelerator
actor
administrator
ambassador
ancestor
arbitrator
auditor
author
aviator
bachelor
benefactor
calculator
captor
censor
chancellor
collaborator
collector
commentator
competitor
conductor
conqueror
conspirator
constructor
contractor
contributor
councillor
counsellor
creator
creditor
curator
debtor
decorator

defector
depositor
dictator
director
distributor
doctor
duplicator
editor
educator
elevator
emperor
equator
escalator
excavator
executor
governor
impostor
incubator
indicator
inheritor
inquisitor
inspector
inventor
investigator
investor
jailor
janitor
legislator
major
mayor
mediator
narrator

navigator
objector
operator
oppressor
orator
pastor
perpetrator
persecutor
predecessor
processor
professor
projector
proprietor
prosecutor
prospector
protector
radiator
rector
reflector
refrigerator
resistor
sailor
senator
solicitor
spectator
sponsor
successor
suitor
supervisor
surveyor
survivor
tailor

tenor	translator	victor
tractor	vendor	visitor
traitor	ventilator	

• *-ar* is used in a few words for people in the sense of doing some particular thing:

| beggar | liar | pedlar |
| burglar | | |

• *-ar* is also used in a few other nouns:

altar	collar	nectar
bursar	dollar	pillar
calendar	grammar	registrar
caterpillar	guitar	scholar
cedar	hangar	vicar
cellar	mortar	vinegar

equally as

The *as* in *equally as* is usually redundant: *equally* alone is enough in comparisons such as the following:

? *They were **equally as** good in the skills of architecture.*
? *You must be in with a good chance, even if other conditions are not **equally as** favourable.*
✓ *They were **equally** good in the skills of architecture.*
✓ *You must be in with a good chance, even if other conditions are not **equally** favourable.*

Useful alternatives are *just as* in positive contexts and *quite so* in negative contexts:

✓ *They were **just as** good in the skills of architecture.*

✓ *You must be in with a good chance, even if other conditions are not **quite so** favourable.*

But you need *as* when it is paired with another *as* in a balanced comparison:

✓ *Bream do not transfer successfully even to a water **equally as** rich **as** the one they came from.*

especially, specially

It is all too possible to use the wrong word inadvertently.

Especially means 'in particular' or 'more than in other cases':

*Public anxiety was **especially** evident in the weeks following these accidents.*

Whereas *specially* means 'for a special purpose':

*Some of the vegetables were **specially** imported all the way from India.*

A common mistake is to use *especially* where *specially* is called for:

✗ *Some of the houses have been designed **especially** for older people.*
✓ *Some of the houses have been designed **specially** for older people.*

euphemisms

Euphemism is the use of a milder or vaguer word or expression in place of one that might seem too harsh or direct, such as (for sexual activity) *make love, sleep together, fallen woman*, (for old age) *senior citizen, sunset years*, and (for death) *to pass away, to face one's maker*.

This kind of softening of reality is sometimes needed to avoid offence or embarrassment. But some forms of euphemism can be unwelcome or even offensive:

• those that obscure or generalize the meaning (e.g. *sexual assault* for *rape*) or cause misunderstanding (e.g. *cloakroom* for *lavatory*)

• those that attempt to make repellent or destructive activities appear harmless or constructive (e.g. *ethnic cleansing* and *population transfer* for the wholesale killing or deportation of peoples)

Some euphemisms have become so much associated with officialdom that they are best avoided in general use, e.g. *exploring every avenue* ('making extensive inquiries'). Others are only suitable in humorous contexts, e.g. *tired and emotional* ('drunk') and *economical with the truth* ('lying').

evade

See AVERT, AVOID, EVADE.

every

See EACH, EVERY.

everyone, every one

As with *anyone* and *any one*, the spelling as one or two words depends on whether the words are intended compositionally, each retaining its separate meaning, or as a unified meaning equivalent to *everybody*:

*He insists that **everyone** in the office should 'get out in the field' occasionally.*
*As **everyone** is aware, world standards are high.*

*Their aim was to visit **every one** of the eight hundred or so families in the parish each year.*
*The Board has to vet **every one** of the artists shown at the exhibition.*

exceedingly, excessively

Exceedingly is equivalent to 'very' or 'extremely', signifying an acceptable extreme or high degree; it is generally a favourable word. *Excessively* on the other hand is typically used unfavourably as an alternative for 'too'; as its form suggests it signifies excess:

*As far as you are concerned, a covenant can be **exceedingly** simple.*
*This **exceedingly** sensible system has not always been applied in an even-handed manner.*

*There are times when this universe seems **excessively**, even arbitrarily, bleak.*

*Rose was **excessively** clinging in her behaviour.*

except

See ACCEPT, EXCEPT.

exceptional, exceptionable

The more useful – and therefore more common – word is *exception*, which is used in the sense 'forming an *exception*, unusual' (typically with favourable or positive implications):

*Gorky – **exceptional** among painters – was a fervent scrutinizer of paintings.*

*There may be **exceptional** circumstances in which the company is unable to produce final figures.*

*The collection is **exceptional** for its quality, value, diversity, and state of conservation.*

Exceptionable, as well as being awkward to say, is awkward in meaning 'likely to cause disagreement, objectionable'. It is found much more commonly in its negative form *unexceptionable* meaning 'beyond criticism, acceptable'. Better alternatives for *exceptionable* are *objectionable*, *disagreeable*, *unpleasant*, *unacceptable*, and *intolerable*.

excoriate

See CORUSCATE, EXCORIATE.

exhaustive, exhausting

Something is *exhaustive* when it exhausts all the possibilities, i.e. it is comprehensive, whereas it is *exhausting* when it exhausts you. An *exhaustive series of tests* is complete and covers all the ground, and is also *exhausting* if it leaves everyone involved fatigued and weary (*exhausted*, in fact). The examples given below will further clarify the meanings:

*These lists are not **exhaustive** – if they were they would fill the entire book.*
*They had planned their movements in **exhaustive** detail.*

*Struggling for breath can be **exhausting** and frightening.*
*She felt as if she'd made a long **exhausting** hike.*

fact (the fact that)

The expression *the fact that* is useful in making clauses into noun phrases:

*We are referring here to **the fact that** capital movements require the exchange of currencies.*

At the start of a sentence, it is possible to reduce *the fact that* to simply *that*, but the emphasis or focus may be lost:

***The fact that** he was a very junior cleric with little political experience limited his ability to mount a serious challenge to the existing leadership.*

Sentences made to depend on *the fact that* can often be recast to their advantage in other ways:

*Equally disturbing was **the fact that** [✓ It was equally disturbing that] the House of Representatives voted narrowly to reject the Bill.*

It is best to avoid using *the fact that* when another *that* precedes:

*It is assumed **that the fact that** teachers and pupils are together in a special classroom implies the presence of an educational programme relevant to the development of children.*

This ungainly sentence can easily be recast as follows:

*It is assumed that **because** teachers and pupils are together in a special classroom there is an educational programme relevant to the development of children.*

Note also that the phrases *owing to the fact that* (or *on account of the fact that*) and *despite the fact that* can normally be replaced by *because* and *although* respectively, producing a much neater and clearer structure:

*? This was **on account of the fact that** [✓ This was because] after the big switch-on of the water power there arose a scare.*

Verbs that can be complemented by a *that*-clause do not need to be linked by *the fact that*, so that in the following sentences *the fact that* can be replaced by *that*:

*? Perhaps it signifies **the fact that** the poem could apply to anyone in life.*

*? Is my honourable friend aware **of the fact that** a German manufacturer has transferred all its operations to my constituency?*

farther, farthest

See FURTHER, FURTHEST, FARTHER, FARTHEST.

fatal, fateful

Both words have to do with the workings of fate, and their meanings have often overlapped. *Fateful* means 'having far-reaching consequences', and unlike *fatal* these might be good or neutral as well as bad. *Fatal* means 'causing death' (*a fatal accident*), and can refer to inanimate things and situations as well as to those that can suffer actual death. So a *fateful journey* is one that affects people in important ways, whereas a *fatal journey* is one that brings death. Useful synonyms to *fatal* in this meaning are *catastrophic*, *disastrous*, and *ruinous*.

feasible

Feasible is often used as an alternative for *possible*, but this is not always correct as its range of meaning is narrower. *Possible* can mean either 'capable of being done' (referring to practicality) or 'likely' (referring to expected outcome), whereas *feasible* properly corresponds only to the first of these meanings, 'capable of being done or carried out' or 'practical':

✓ *Mass screening is not **feasible**, although targeting groups at high risk is a realistic proposition.*
✓ *An uninterruptible power source was thought to be the only **feasible** answer.*

Feasible is not a valid alternative to *possible* when it means 'likely' or 'probable':

✗ It is **feasible** [✓ *likely* or *probable*] *that the Greeks were more sharp-sighted than we are.*

✗ *A surprise win remains a* **feasible** [✓ *possible*] *outcome.*

The same is true of the adverb *feasibly*, which means 'in a way that is practical' (a meaning also shared by *possibly*). It is not a substitute for *possibly* in its sense 'as is likely':

✓ *This reform could only* **feasibly** *be carried out within companies by single employers.*

✗ *There's one way in which the authorities could* **feasibly** [✓ *possibly* or *reasonably*] *have acted more promptly.*

> Lear is essentially impossible to be represented on a stage. But how many dramatic personages are there in Shakespeare, which though more tractable and feasible (if I may so speak) than Lear, yet from some circumstance, some adjunct to their character, are improper to be shewn to our bodily eye.
>
> Charles Lamb, *On the Tragedies of Shakespeare*, 1818

fetus, foetus

Fetus is now the more common spelling in medical use in Britain and the USA, in accordance with the word's origin (Latin *fetus* meaning 'offspring'). *Fetus* is becoming dominant in general use in Britain, despite the misconceived notion that this spelling is an Americanism; but *foetus* is still common. The corresponding adjective is *fetal*, with *foetal* becoming less common in BrE even in general use.

fewer

See LESS *AND* FEWER.

fictional, fictitious

Fictional means 'occurring in fiction', i.e. in a piece of literature, whereas *fictitious* means 'invented, unreal; not genuine'. So *Oliver Twist* is a *fictional* name when it refers to Dickens's character, and a *fictitious* name when someone uses it as a false or assumed name instead of their own. Similarly, events are *fictional* when described in a work of fiction, and *fictitious* when invented in ordinary life.

flagrant

See BLATANT, FLAGRANT.

flammable

See INFLAMMABLE, FLAMMABLE.

flat, flatly

The adverb *flatly*, formed from *flat*, is used only in two figurative meanings, the first more common than the second:

• 'completely, without reservation' to intensify words expressing refusal, rejection, denial, contradiction, and so on (typically coming before the verb, though occasionally following it as in the last example below):

*They **flatly** refused to relinquish their grip on power.*
*He **flatly** rejected the pleas of Aung San to stand for election.*
*In his statement he **flatly** denied any illicit trading.*
*The opposition parties have energy policies that are **flatly** contradicted by their environmental policies.*
*She had refused **flatly** to consider him as her groom.*

• 'in a dull way' with reporting verbs such as *say, speak, tell, inform,* and so on:

*'Oh, I did that,' she told him **flatly**.*

Sometimes the two senses identified above overlap, giving an impression of both:

*'It's your choice,' he retorted **flatly**, and looked at his watch.*

Flat has a role halfway between adjective and adverb, but more the first than the second, when it means 'in (or into) a flat position':

*The mirror was placed **flat** against the wall.*
*The edges of the paper are bent **flat**.*

Flat is used as an adverb in a few special cases such as *flat broke, flat out,* and *to turn something down flat*:

*I was going to be **flat broke** in a couple of days.*
*A pair of reed warblers work **flat out** to keep the young cuckoo satisfied.*
*He **turned down flat** the king's ransom, the pot of gold, the answer to his prayers.*

flaunt, flout

These words are easy to confuse because their forms are close and their meanings are in the same semantic domain.

Flaunting something, usually a quality or attribute, is parading it ostentatiously:

*His mother had always **flaunted** his poverty as if it were a virtue.*

Flouting is disregarding or treating institutions with contempt, typically rules, laws, conventions, principles, expectations, etc.:

*Many parents are **flouting** the rear-seatbelt laws and leaving their children unrestrained in cars.*
*If too many expectations are **flouted**, the writer might be suspected of being unbalanced.*

forbear, forebear

Forbear is a verb (past *forbore*, past participle *forborne*) and means 'to restrain oneself from doing something' (*forbore to answer back*). A *forebear* (based on the element *fore-*) is an ancestor and is typically used in the plural (*had no knowledge of their forebears*). The noun is occasionally also spelt *forbear*, but this is not good practice.

forego, forgo

To *forego* is to go in front or before; it is mostly used in the form *foregoing* (as in *read the foregoing carefully*) and in the past participle *foregone* in the expression *foregone conclusion*, a conclusion that is inevitable and so in a sense has 'gone before'. To *forgo* something is to abstain from it or do without it; typically one forgoes a right or privilege, or something else desirable (*We are being asked to forgo all these advantages*).

forever, for ever

Forever tends to be spelt as one word as an adverb meaning 'constantly' or 'incessantly', usually in un-favourable contexts (*is forever complaining*). As two words, *for ever* means 'for all time' (*events that changed the world for ever*).

former *and* latter

In their complementary meanings, *former* refers to the first of two people or things mentioned and *latter* to the second. They can both be used either alone as nouns (usually as *the former* and *the latter*) or as modifiers before other nouns (*the former person, the latter thing*):

*Although the land was meant to be divided between Romans and barbarians, many of the **former** were forcibly ejected.*
*Later, Edward was to settle in Israel, where he engaged in building projects in Tel Aviv and undertook to constuct a new city centre in Jerusalem. This **latter** project is now on hold.*

When they are used together contrastively in the same sentence they are usually nouns:

*We waded into the living room, where just a small stream flowed through from the area of the guest bedroom and bathroom. The **former** was dry, but the **latter** was gradually catching up with the kitchen.*

> *Dr P., through long acquaintance with many of the ills flesh is heir to, had acquired a somewhat trying habit of regarding a man and his wound as separate institutions, and seemed rather annoyed that the former should express any opinion upon the latter, or claim any right in it, while under his care.*
>
> Louisa May Alcott, *Hospital Sketches*, 1863

Former and *latter* should not be used in this way when more than two items have been mentioned:

✗ *J B Danquah, half-brother of a paramount chief, was the moving spirit, along with Akufo Addo, a close relative of Danquah, Obetsibi Lamptey, from Accra, Ako Adjei, and now Nkrumah. All except the **latter** [✓ the last or the last named] were lawyers.*

It is also usually poor style to use *former* or *latter* when the items they refer to are ill-defined or positioned a long way back in the sentence, requiring the reader to pause and backtrack in order to make the link:

*Later trackways involved large quantities of coppiced poles and rails (as in the hurdles used in the Walton Heath track) and, in the Meare Heath trackway, a reused timber structure – possibly a house. The **former** indicates that areas of woodland were being carefully managed as coppices with standards in the*

Neolithic and Bronze Ages to produce the poles for rails and hurdles and the timber for the heavier tracks.

Note that both words have meanings not shared correspondingly by the other:

• *Former* has a meaning to which *latter* does not correspond, namely 'having been previously but no longer':

*Ambitious plans to turn a **former** biscuit factory into an Olympic venue risk failure because it is in the wrong place.*
*Tim, a **former** head boy at Richmond School, got his geography degree at Liverpool last summer.*

• *Latter* has a meaning to which *former* does not correspond, denoting the last stage or stages of a process or the most recent part of a period of time (as in *latter-day* denoting a modern equivalent of something older):

*I don't want in this **latter** stage of my career to be pushed out of what little limelight I had.*
*By the **latter** part of the nineteenth century there were two aspects of the popularization of science.*
*Do we really want our daughters to become **latter-day** Amazons?*

fortunate / fortuitous

*It was **fortunate** [= useful, beneficial] that I had a good friend of my own age.*
*It was entirely **fortuitous** [= accidental, coincidental] that the aircraft involved was a Boeing 707.*

These words are related (via Latin *fortuna*) in different uses of our word *fortune*. *Fortunate* means 'having good fortune', and signifies good luck or advantage, whereas *fortuitous* means 'occurring by chance' and implies mere accident or coincidence. A *fortuitous discovery* is one that is accidental or random, whereas a *fortunate discovery* is one that brings benefits and has a good outcome.

Beware of using *fortuitous* when you mean *fortunate*:

✗ It was **fortuitous** [✓ fortunate, lucky] *for me that I was about the right age for the part.*

It was **fortuitous** [= accidental, coincidental] *that Christies had sent the Van Gogh on a pre-auction tour of Japan.*
The results are based on a **fortunate** [= useful, beneficial] *discovery made in 1968.*

The same distinction applies to the corresponding adverbs *fortuitously* and *fortunately*:

Fortunately [= luckily, by good fortune], *there had been time to buy a half bottle of whisky on the way to the station.*
Most people had, **fortuitously** [= by chance, as it happens], *travelled the night before.*
All this happened while the principal beneficiary was **fortuitously** [= by chance] *out of the room.*
Fortunately [= by good chance], *the house was empty when the bomb exploded.*

> *Close upon the hour of ten every morning the fortuitous meeting of two gentlemen at Mrs. Warwick's housedoor was a signal for punctiliously stately greetings, the*

*salutation of the raised hat and a bow of the head from
a position of military erectness.*

George Meredith, Diana of the Crossways, 1885

fulsome

*Mary Brotherton did not believe a word of it, and sick
of the false and fulsome flattery that was bandied about
between the knight, the lady, and the poet, she made, as
we have seen, a somewhat hasty retreat.*

Frances Trollope, The Life and Adventures of Michael Armstrong, 1840

This is a word that has changed from being complimentary to disapproving and (almost) back again. It
originally meant 'copious or abundant', but by the
sixteenth century it had developed unfavourable overtones suggesting excess rather than generosity, which
are also found in nineteenth-century writing (as above)
and which it now has only occasionally.

More recently, a positive and complimentary meaning has reappeared:

? *The* Times *obituary was* **fulsome** *in praise of his achievements.*

Although the meaning is clear enough in this kind of
usage, it will sometimes grate with readers, because the
word still carries several hundred years of unpleasant
overtones. It is therefore sometimes best to use an
alternative word such as *profuse*, *lavish*, *enthusiastic*,
generous, and *liberal*.

✓ *The* Times *obituary was generous* [or *lavish*] *in praise of his
achievements.*

? *There was a heavy irony in Lady Thatcher's **fulsome** [✓ generous] tribute to the women who had campaigned for the vote.*

? *He had not returned any **fulsome** [✓ profuse or lavish or enthusiastic] gratitude to his staff for all the work they had put in during the day.*

further, furthest, farther, farthest

Further and *furthest* are the older forms, dating from Old English, and are also the more common forms in current usage, especially in generalized senses not involving physical distance:

*Nothing could be **further** from costume drama or the spreading of cloaks over puddles.*
*These skills are **further** encouraged and developed in a workshop environment.*
*The **furthest** thing from my mind was that I'd be a clothing manufacturer.*

Farther and *farthest* tend to be used more when they refer to physical distance. The reason for this may be their apparent closeness to the word *far*, but they are only coincidentally related to it and not derived from it:

*He heard an excited voice **farther** down the track.*
*They watched the crow clear the **farther** hedge and disappear into the wood.*
*Dora was sitting alone in the **farthest** corner of the room.*
*There seemed to be a door cut into the wall that was **farthest** away from the window.*

Further or *furthest* could be substituted in all the above examples.

Further is the only choice in certain contexts:

• when it as an adjective meaning 'additional', as in the following examples:

*Our region is poised for **further** growth once the election is out of the way.*
*If you require any **further** help please contact me.*

• when it is an adverb meaning 'additionally, for a longer time':

*She found she had answered before she had given herself time to think **further**.*

• when it is a sentence adverb meaning 'moreover' or 'what is more':

*Cinema, **further**, more than any other cultural product, has been structured around sexuality.*

• when it is a verb meaning 'to promote or advance an idea, scheme, etc.':

*It is now not uncommon for wives to decide to stay put in order to **further** their own careers.*

gamble, gambol

These two words have no connection in meaning but their spellings can be confused. Both are nouns as well as verbs.

To *gamble* is to make bets or wagers (with the derivative verbal noun *gambling*); to *gambol* is to run or leap around playfully and is typically used of animals and young children and is common figuratively:

Boyfriend and girlfriend fall in love. For several months, they **gambol** *through life like spring lambs.*

gender *and* gender-neutrality

It has become much more important in recent years to avoid offending sensitivities regarding gender in language. This is a social issue as much as linguistic, but there are one or two language traps to avoid in preserving gender-neutrality:

• It is a well-established and legitimate practice to use plural pronouns to avoid having to specify gender in sentences such as the following:

I mean freedom in the broader sense of each individual having the freedom to develop **their** *potential to the full.*

> *Whenever a person says to you that they are as innocent as can be in all concerning money, look well after your own money, for they are dead certain to collar it, if they can.*
>
> Charles Dickens, *Bleak House*, 1853

If you use *he or she*, *his or her*, and so on, which are also legitimate but can become cumbersome, there is sometimes a problem of sustaining the options throughout a longer sentence, and it is important to avoid a mixed inconsistency:

✗ *Whatever happens, you must protect your relationship with your child and let* **him or her** *know that you still love* **them**.

The writer might as well have opted for the plural pronoun from the start:

✓ *Whatever happens, you must protect your relationship with your child and let* **them** *know that you still love* **them**.

• Avoid mixtures of styles when referring to men and women in the same context, e.g. use *men and women* (or *boys and girls*) and not *men and girls*.

• Gender-specific names for occupations, such as *comedienne* and *usherette*, and many words ending in -*ess*, are much less used and can easily be avoided, except when the sex of the person named is significant (as with *actress*). A few are surviving, notably *manageress* when referring to a woman in charge of a restaurant or hotel.

(This entry has concentrated on possible errors. For a fuller discussion of gender-neutrality see *How to Write Better English*, pp. 206–10.)

genteelisms

A genteelism is a seemingly more polite word borrowed from formal or technical usage and used in place of a word that is considered distasteful, improper, or simply vulgar. They are in fact euphemisms taken a stage further and forced into an inappropriate language register. Attitudes to this type of usage vary from generation to generation, and some that were formerly disapproved of seem no longer to offend today. A few remaining examples include *desire* for *want*, *endeavour* for *try*, *hard of hearing* for *deaf*, *enquire* for *ask*, *peruse* for *read*, *perspire* for *sweat*, and phrases such as *retire for the night* for *go to bed*. On the whole they are best avoided.

get

This is one of the commonest and most useful words in English, and it is a pity that so many hang-ups have developed over its use. In particular, it is quite acceptable at all levels of writing to use *get* in place of *be* to form passives, especially to emphasize process or development as distinct from situation or result:

*Her clothes **were** soaked when she got home* (result).
*Her clothes **got** soaked on the way home* (process).

It is also perfectly good English to use *get* in place of *obtain*, *acquire*, *purchase*, and other genteelisms sometimes proposed. *Get* can also mean 'arrive' (*we got home late*).

The past participle of *get* is *got* in BrE. In AmE another form *gotten*, preserved from older English, is also used when there is some element of acquisition or development. Americans would say *we have gotten an apartment in Manhattan* when they mean they have recently moved in, and *we have got an apartment in Manhattan* (or more likely, *we have an apartment . . .*) when they are talking about their present situation.

gorilla, guerrilla

The two words sound almost the same. *Gorilla* is the large ape; a *guerrilla* (a Spanish word from *guerra* meaning 'war') is a member of an independent fighting force. (It can also be spelt *guerilla*, but the form given in the headword is preferable.)

graffiti

This word for daubings on a wall is an Italian plural form (meaning 'scratches'). It used to be the preserve of art historians and archaeologists referring to drawings or writing on the walls of ancient buildings such famously as those at Pompeii. In recent years the spread of spray-can daubing on walls has given the term a much wider currency, causing it to be generally accepted as a mass noun like *confetti* or *spaghetti*, with associated verbs and pronouns in the singular:

*Along the towpath we met almost nobody and there **was** no **graffiti**.*
***One graffiti** showed a naked woman.*
(Purists might prefer to write One of the graffiti . . . or One piece of the graffiti . . .)

Very often it is impossible to tell whether the word is being treated as singular or plural because the associated grammar is identical:

*The new initiative is aimed at showing how young people can use **graffiti** as art.*

The singular *graffito* is rarely used except in technical contexts.

had rather

> *This would not be an ordinary picnic; it would be like a little romance to me, and I had rather have it than any birthday present you could give me.*

Louisa May Alcott, *Moods*, 1865

This literary use in the eighteenth and nineteenth centuries of *had rather* in place of *would* (or *should*) *rather* is sometimes still heard in informal speech. The modern use, which may be a revival rather than a survival, is probably due to the similar sound the two forms *had* and *would* can have in ordinary conversation. *Had rather* is now non-standard and should be avoided:

✗ *I **had rather** [✓ would rather] be at the bottom of the River Thames than one week in debt.*

half

Half is a noun (*the first half of the book / there is still another half left*), an adjective (*a half share*) and an adverb (*had half promised to help*). It is also a so-called 'predeterminer', i.e. it can be placed before another determiner such as *a* and *the*, as in *half a mile away* and *took half the morning*). It is a mistake to use *a* before *half* as well, tempting though this sometimes is when the word after *half* is *a* or *an*: ✗ *The house was a half an hour's walk away.*

When *half* is followed by a singular noun (with or without *of* between), the verb is also singular:

***Half** that amount is enough.*

When the noun is plural the verb is plural:

***Half** the people who voted want to join the organization.*
***Half** of the tins were packed in cases of 24.*

When *half* or *half of* is followed by a collective noun

with a strong plural implication, a plural verb can follow:

Half the workforce are involved in making integrated circuit modules.
Half the crowd expect a punk band.

hangar, hanger

A *hangar* is a large shed for housing aircraft; a *hanger* is a device for hanging clothes in a cupboard.

hanged, hung

The usual past tense and past participle of the verb *hang* is *hung*:

*They **hung** about and then came on here.*
*Over his shoulder was **hung** a canvas bag.*

In the sense to do with capital punishment, the form used is *hanged*:

*The SS **hanged** him at Flossenburg concentration camp in April.*
*The swaying corpse of the **hanged** man caught his glance.*

A *hung council* or *parliament* is one in which no single party has an overall majority to take power.

hanging participles

See PARTICIPLES.

hardly

See BARELY, HARDLY, SCARCELY.

have

As an auxiliary verb, *have* forms the perfect tenses of other verbs (*they have spoken*), and its own past tense *had* forms the so-called past perfect (or pluperfect: *they had spoken*). It is also used to form conditional sentences, i.e. sentences with an *if* in them:

If I had known that, I would not have been so angry.
It would have been better if they had not said anything.

Do not make the mistake of adding in a redundant *have*, which you sometimes see in carelessly written letters and news reports:

✗ *If I had have known that, I would have acted differently.*
✗ *It would have been better if we had not have said anything.*

here is / are, there is / are

When the noun following *here* or *there* is singular the verb is the singular form *is* (or *was* for the past):

Here is [or Here's] a list of items it would be wise to keep in your cupboard.

When the noun following is plural the verb is the plural form *are* (or *were* for the past):

There are exemptions for gifts to spouses.

A sum of money or other amount is often treated as if singular although the grammatical form might be plural:

Here is *£50 for expenses.*
(*Here are £50 for expenses* is grammatical but less idiomatic in ordinary speaking.)

In casual conversation a sentence such as *Here's some flowers for you* is idiomatic and acceptable, but not in writing and other more formal contexts.

hers

There is no apostrophe: *this work of hers.*

historic, historical

Both words describe people and things 'to do with history', i.e. from the past or connected with the past. *Historical* is a more objective classifying word that refers to something that existed or happened in the past, whereas *historic* describes what has an important role in the past and means 'famous or important in history'. A meeting, for example, is described as *historical* to distinguish one that is known to have happened from one that is or may be fictitious, whereas a *historic* meeting is one that is of great importance in history (as opposed to one that is unimportant). *Historic* is often used with reference to buildings and monuments. When the wrong choice is made, it is usually *historic* that is used when *historical* would be better (e.g. *historic evidence* instead of *historical evidence*).

homogeneous, homogenous

Homogeneous (with the stress on the third syllable) means 'of the same kind, forming a consistent whole':

*Users are not a **homogeneous** group and their needs may conflict.*

Homogenous (stressed on the second syllable) is a word in biology meaning 'having a common descent'. It is more often found misused for *homogeneous*:

✗ *In more **homogenous** countries than Italy and Belgium, proportional representation does not prevent absolute majorities being won.*

The adjective *homogenized*, denoting milk that has been treated to prevent the cream from separating, is related in form but not in meaning.

hopefully

See ADVERBS: *sentence adverbs*.

however

There are three points on which *however* can cause trouble:

• when to spell it as two words rather than one (as with *what ever* and *when ever*)
• whether it can come at the beginning of a sentence when it means 'on the other hand'
• whether to use a comma, or two commas, or none

You use two words when *how* is asking a question intensified by *ever*, in the same way as *where ever* and *when ever*. As a guide, see if you can substitute *how on earth* for *how ever*: if you can, as in both the following examples, you spell it as two words:

How ever will you persuade them?
How ever did these items get put in the fridge?

However is written as one word in its contrasting meaning 'on the other hand' and when it means 'in whatever way' or 'to whatever extent':

However you regard these theories, they have never been adhered to for long.
However many problems there may be, there is a natural instinct to form relationships all through our lives.

However, we are mainly concerned here with *however* in the sense 'on the other hand', as it does at the beginning of this sentence. The view that *however* cannot come at the beginning of a sentence is a superstition. In fact, *however* is extremely mobile within a sentence, and choice of position is determined by the varying need for emphasis and sentence balance. At the beginning of a sentence, it will have the effect of emphasizing the following contrast or reservation more forcefully:

However, it would be wrong to dismiss this line of thought entirely.
However, many problems still remain, and we need to address them.

When *however* comes at the beginning of a sentence,

as in the two examples above, the comma that follows
it is important, not just in indicating the pause that
normally follows, but in clarifying the meaning. Without the comma in the second sentence a reader might
think, even if only momentarily, that you are going to
say *however many problems still remain* in the alternative sense 'regardless of how many problems remain',
with a continuation such as 'we can succeed in dealing
with them'. Notice the difference between the first
example (with a comma) and the second example
(without a comma) in each of the pairs that follow:

***However**, the results are coordinated and published in the next
issue of the journal.*
***However** [= in whatever way] the results are coordinated, the
outlook is not bright.*
***However**, few people would subscribe to this opinion today.*
***However** few [= regardless of how few] people would subscribe
to this opinion today, it has been influential in the past.*

The continuation of the sentence normally makes the
meaning clear; but the momentary ambiguity it can
cause the reader is best avoided.

Placed later in the sentence, *however* has a generally
milder effect. In this position, because *however* is a
kind of aside embracing the whole sentence, there
should be commas before and after it:

*Many problems, **however**, still remain.*
*The ombudsman cannot, **however**, investigate a complaint that
is already subject to court proceedings.*
*They may be reluctant to take their idea to another. An idea or
invention, **however**, is like someone's child.*

(Note that the same rule about commas applies to *though*, which cannot be used at the beginning of a sentence in this type of use:

*It is true, **though**, that we have never treated the Royal Family with that hysterical mixture of reverence and prurience that some newspapers seem to think the badge of a loyal subject.*)

Finally, *however* (as well as *though* in informal use) can be placed at the end of a sentence (with an optional comma), where its impact is weakest:

*Many problems still remain, **however**.*
*Giving him his liberty would not cancel his debt **however**.*

human, humane, humanitarian

Human is a noun (*no humans left alive*) as well as an adjective (*a human body / a human response*), whereas *humane* is only an adjective. As an adjective, *human* mainly classifies physical words to do with the body and people, e.g. *behaviour, being, body, life, mind, nature, race, rights,* and *speech*. It also has a judgemental meaning, implying either weakness or limitation (*human failings / is only human*) or more positive aspects (*a very human reaction / strong human under-standing*).

In its positive judgemental meaning *human* overlaps with *humane*. A key difference is that *human* denotes qualities that distinguish human behaviour from that of non-humans, whereas *humane* is to do with the way people treat each other:

*Lloyd George was a man with profound **human** qualities.*

*She looked at him with a very **human** suspicion.*

*The relief of the small-town poor seems to have been based on a **humane** assessment of need and sufficient relief.*
*We must seek a more **humane** way of keeping families together.*

Humane can be used about the good treatment of animals as well as of other people:

*The animals must be reared in **humane** conditions.*
*The only **humane** option was for the dog to be put to sleep, a court heard.*

Humanitarian has a special meaning 'relating to the promotion of human welfare' in contexts such as *international aid, relief, concern, intervention, mission, organization, work*, etc. In more recent use it has taken on a wider meaning in relation to conflict and catastrophe, as in *humanitarian crisis, disaster*, etc., where the sense 'requiring humanitarian action' is effectively the opposite of the original one. Because combinations such as these can constitute grotesque contradictions in terms, care is needed in using the word.

hung

See HANGED, HUNG.

I *and* me, *and other pronoun confusion*

There are several areas of uncertainty about whether to say *you and me* or *you and I* (or *him and I* or *him and me*, and other pairs) after the verb *be* and after prepositions, in particular *between*:

• *between you and I*

✘ *There's really little difference* **between you and I** [✓ me] *struggling to count on our fingers, and the most modern and sophisticated piece of computing wizardry.*

✘ *During the crisis emails were passing* **between the bosses and he** [✓ him] *practically hourly.*

In the first sentence, *me* and not *I* is the correct form, and in the second sentence *him* and not *he*, since *between* governs both *you* and *me* in the first and both *the bosses* and *him* in the second. *I* and *he* are the forms used for the subject of a sentence.

• *at, for,* and other prepositions

Me and not *I* is needed:

✘ *The students were waiting for their teacher and* **I** [✓ me].

The reason is clear if you take out the first part of the object:

✘ *The students were waiting for* **I**.
✓ *The students were waiting for* **me**.

• after the verb *be*

After the verb *be* (*am, is, are,* etc.) you can use both the subjective form of the pronoun (*I, we,* etc.) and the objective form (*me, us,* etc.); the objective forms are more natural and usual in ordinary spoken English:

She said it would only be **her** *coming.*
That's **us** *looking out of the window.*
Is it **him** *you want to meet?*

The subjective forms can sound affected and un-idiomatic, especially when they are repeated in the same sentence or when the first-person forms *I* and *we* are involved:

? *She said it would only be **she** coming.*
? *That's **we** looking out of the window.*

It is, however, usual to use the subjective forms when a relative clause (introduced by *who* or *that*) follows:

✓ *It was **I** who said that.* (*It was me who said it* and, especially
? *It was me that said it,* have a much more informal ring.)

-ible

See -ABLE, -IBLE.

iconic

This has become one of the more tedious vogue words of recent years: tedious because it is so frequently used (especially in journalism and broadcasting) that one tires of it. This is a poor way to treat a potentially powerful and effective word. It is based on the noun *icon*, a term originally (and still) used to mean a holy picture but now probably more familiar with reference to a small symbol on a VDU screen. The modern meaning is 'important or influential as typifying a culture, movement, etc.'; all too often however it is used in a grossly diluted sense 'significant, famous', which is a waste of a good word:

? *More than 80 members and guests enjoyed an informative evening, and explored this vibrant and **iconic** cultural building.*

? *She was offered big roles in Hollywood. 'It was an incredibly **iconic** time for me. I loved making the movie.'*

What *iconic* can possibly mean in the second of these examples is anyone's guess.

-ie- *or* -ei-

The spelling of words containing the vowel group -ie- or -ei- always causes problems. The rule '*i* before *e* except after *c*' applies only to words pronounced with an -ee- sound (e.g. *brief, chief, grief, hygiene, siege* but *deceive, perceive, receive*). When it is pronounced -ay- or -iy-, the spelling is more usually -ei- (e.g. *eight, feign, heir, neighbour, reign, vein, weigh; either, height, seismology, sleight of hand*). Note also *leisure*, and words such as *hierarchy* and *patient* in which the two vowels are separately pronounced or form a diphthong.

Exceptions to the rule as defined above are *caffeine, codeine, protein, seize, weir,* and *weird*. Note especially *seize* and *siege*, which are often misspelt.

For a fuller discussion of this topic, see George Davidson, *Improve Your Spelling* in this series.

if and when

'Any writer who uses this formula lays himself open to entirely reasonable suspicions on the part of his readers

> *. . . There is the suspicion that he has merely been too*
> *lazy to make up his mind between* if *and* when.'
>
> H. W. Fowler, *A Dictionary of Modern English Usage*, 1926

These strictures may sound dated, but the advice still has some value. You will not go far wrong if you regard *if and when* as an avoidable cliché but, like most clichés, it can be effective in the right place. The following examples distinguish what is useful from what is merely decorative or redundant:

✓ *They want to be able to act **if and when** they choose.*
   (Both words have equal force: they want to be able to choose both *whether* to act and *when* to act.)
✓ *Our main concern is **if and when** interest rates change.*
   (This is fine because the time is a factor here as well as the possibility.)
? *She should be ready to pick up the pieces **if and when** required.*
   (*If* is adequate here.)
? *The Prince inherited it on becoming Prince of Wales, and will lose it **if and when** he becomes king.*
   (Since the Prince of Wales is heir apparent, *when* alone is adequate.)
? *Do something **if and when** it feels right.*
   (Avoid prevarication and choose!)
? *If you are not ready to deal with the problem **if and when** it occurs, you could be faced with a crisis.*
   (Delete 'if and when it occurs', which adds nothing.)

illegal, illicit

Illegal means 'against the law' (*Overt sex or race discrimination is illegal*), whereas *illicit* relates to rules or customs more generally (*illicit dealing with foreign powers* / *went outside for an illicit cigarette*).

illusion

See ALLUSION, REFERENCE, ILLUSION, DELUSION.

immoral

See AMORAL, IMMORAL.

immune to / from

The basic meaning of *immune* is 'free from the effects or consequences of', and there are two main strands of meaning that follow from this, with the link words *to* and *from* respectively:

• You normally use *immune to* when it refers to disease, or to some other form of attack or risk of harm compared to this:

*Being fearless is like being **immune to** pain.*
*I'm particularly **immune to** crocodile tears.*
*Even though I thought myself **immune to** surprises, what happened next came as something of a shock.*
*They were not **immune to** public pressure nor to the machinations of some of their fellow councillors.*

• You normally use *immune from* when it refers to some kind of obligation or liability (especially a legal one):

*The project has not been totally **immune from** this criticism.*

*Few of us are **immune from** envy.*
*Members of the last parliament were not **immune from** prosecution for corruption even if they had been re-elected.*

The distinction is not watertight, because the concepts overlap. In the first example above, for example, we could justify using *immune to* instead of *immune from*, on the grounds that 'criticism' fits in the 'attacking' category as much as it does the 'obligation' category.

impractical, impracticable

The difference in meaning corresponds to that between the positive forms *practical* and *practicable*.

Impracticable means 'not able to be done or used', is typically used of actions or undertakings, and is primarily factual or informational:

*The walks to most alternative pubs nearby were either too steep or unsafe and **impracticable** for many people.*

Impractical means 'not able to be done sensibly or practically', is more judgemental, and can also be applied to a person in the sense 'not good at doing practical things':

*The gas reserves were previously perceived to be either stranded, too remotely offshore, or **impractical** for development.*
*He clearly believes that it would be **impractical** to ban the song just because of the word 'suicidal', even though it is used repeatedly.*
*He does acknowledge their concern at his **impractical** nature.*

See also PRACTICAL, PRACTICABLE.

inapt, inept

These words are close in meaning but there is a clear distinction. *Inapt* means 'inappropriate or unsuitable' (*an inapt response*), whereas *inept* means 'unskilful or clumsy' (*is embarrassingly inept at household tasks*). An *inept intervention* is one that is bungled; an *inapt intervention* is one that should not have been made at all.

incredible, incredulous

The distinction in meaning between these two words corresponds to that for *credible* and *credulous*. Something that is *incredible* cannot easily be believed, whereas the less common word *incredulous* is used of a person in the sense 'unwilling or unable to believe'. *Incredible* also has an informal meaning 'outstanding' or 'excellent' (*an incredible achievement*).

infer, imply

To *infer* something is to reach a conclusion about it from evidence, such as facts or a statement that you have read or heard. The evidence *implies* or 'suggests', and you *infer* or 'conclude':

✓ *From the above argument a simple hypothesis can **be inferred**.*
✓ *They are not bound to answer questions, and we should not **infer** guilt from any failure to respond.*
✓ *Surely marriage and prostitution are separate and it would be wrong to **infer** that they thrive on one another.*

✓ *The essential nature of a stem cell is that it is self-renewing and, as its name **implies**, the source of other cells.*

✓ *An advertisement **may imply** that, if you love your family/ children/cat/dog, you'll give them product X.*

As can happen with words that describe the same process from different perspectives, in this case the process of drawing conclusions, the role of one has encroached on the other, and in modern use you will often find *infer* used to mean 'imply' or 'suggest' rather than 'deduce' or 'conclude' (but not the other way round: *imply* is not used to mean 'infer'). This development is widely disliked because it obscures the distinction between the two sides of the thinking process outlined above and makes it difficult to be sure what is meant:

✗ *These songs, as I **have** already **inferred** [✓ implied or suggested], are unremarkable.*

✗ *Are you **inferring** [✓ implying or suggesting] that Thomas the Tank Engine is a video nasty?*

✗ *Similar craft were discovered in North America, Iraq, Vietnam, and India. This does not **infer** [✓ imply or mean] that Julius Caesar and his mates flew around the globe in a Lear jet stopping off in a few disparate countries.*

In all these sentences, *imply* or *suggest* should be substituted in the meaning needed.

Because of the obscured or fuzzy meaning *infer* can have, it is sometimes better to avoid it – even though you would be using it correctly – in cases where both the correct and the incorrect meaning could be understood by your readers:

? *It should not be inferred* [✓ *implied* or *concluded*, as appropriate] *that this is a simple trend.*

? *Are employment figures alone sufficient to* **infer** [✓ *conclude* or *suggest*, as appropriate] *that the economy has shifted from a goods to a service economy?*

infinitives

See SPLIT INFINITIVES.

inflammable, flammable

It is important to note that *inflammable* is not the opposite of *flammable*; both words have the same meaning, 'able to catch fire'. The opposite is *non-flammable*, which is typically used of suitably protected fabrics.

inflict

See AFFLICT, INFLICT.

ingenious, ingenuous

Ingenious means 'clever and well thought-out' (*an ingenious solution to the problem*), whereas the less common word *ingenuous* means 'innocent and open, honest' (*possessed an ingenuous self-assurance*; it is perhaps more familiar in its negative form *disingenuous*).

innumerable

The word means 'too many to be counted': avoid using it in contexts that do not support the notion:

✗ *This lack of topographical information is astonishing when one thinks of the **innumerable** [✓ numerous] ancient towns of England that richly deserve such a study.*
(The ancient towns of England can be listed and therefore readily counted.)

See also COUNTLESS.

insure

See ASSURE, ENSURE, INSURE.

intense, intensive

Intense is the choice here in the broad meaning 'existing in a high degree, extreme' as applied to feelings and qualities, and to people in the sense 'apt to feel strong emotion'. It goes typically with words such as *feeling, pleasure, emotion, pressure, rivalry, competition, cold, pain,* etc.

Intensive has narrowed its scope in modern usage to the sense 'directed to a single point or objective, thorough, vigorous':

*Through its **intensive** training programme, the Centre aims to produce well-trained scholars to undertake research on outstanding problems in this rapidly developing field.*

It also occurs in the special terms *intensive care* (of

medical treatment) and *labour-intensive* (in the sense 'needing a large workforce').

interment, internment

These words are used only occasionally and are therefore liable to confusion, often with absurd results. *Interment* (from the verb *inter*) is the burial of a dead person; *internment* (from the verb *intern*) is the confinement of a living person in a prison or detention camp, typically in wartime.

inured

Becoming *inured to* a thing or a person means growing accustomed or used to them, unpleasant or unwelcome and difficult though they are. Note that the thing can be a verbal noun ending in *-ing*:

*The swimmers, by now **inured** to the ritual humiliation of walking through public spaces dressed only in intimate apparel, have a new challenge: how to keep their mouths closed for 70m while swimming across a boating lake.*
*Is society so **inured** to bad parenting that the demarcation between right and wrong has become nebulous?*

It is not a synonym for 'immune', and the verb *inure* is not a synonym for 'protect':

✗ *We are all **inured** against newspaper headlines.*
✗ *We have the Birmingham Six and the Guildford Four to **inure** us against claims by authority that individuals are lying subversives.*

invaluable

This means 'extremely valuable' (originally, having a value too high to be estimated: *an invaluable experience / invaluable support*) and is not an opposite of *valuable*. For this, use *valueless* (*an opinion that proved valueless*).

ironic, ironical

These two adjectives based on the noun *irony* mean much the same, and choice between them is largely a matter of rhythm and balance in the sentence. *Irony*, the root word, is the expression of an idea or thought by words that normally mean the opposite, or in a manner that normally conveys the opposite. (In the theatre, dramatic irony arises when the audience is aware of a significant fact which one or more of the participants in the drama does not know, causing dramatic tension.) To say *what a lovely day* when looking out on pouring rain is a form of irony, and the statement is ironic; to laugh when you are angry is to react in a way that is *ironic*:

*An **ironical** smile played over her features.*
*'I wonder just how helpful you are being.' She paused to stress his name with **ironic** friendliness.*
*The announcement was made in tones that most observers took to be **ironical**.*

This meaning has developed to describe facts and circumstances that convey the notion of a paradox, or the opposite of what you might expect:

*It is **ironic** that some of the most severe weather conditions can produce the most intricate and beautiful sights.*
*It was **ironical** that the man she had just rebuked should be the only one who had shown interest in her as a woman during the fifteen months she had been on the station.*

Some language purists question this second meaning, but it is well established and since it does not compromise the earlier meaning it is acceptable, although *paradoxical* is often an effective alternative.

its, it's

This pair of words, distinguished only by an apostrophe, is the cause of one of the most common errors in English writing. *Its* (without apostrophe) is the possessive form of *it* (*the largest of its kind*), whereas *it's* is a contracted form of *it is* or *it has* (*it's nice to be here* / *it's been nice staying here*).

-ize, -ise

Verbs in English that end in *-ize* (and corresponding nouns in *-ization*) can often also be spelt with *-ise* (and *-isation*), a form that is historically derived from French rather than directly from the Greek words that give the spelling with *z*. Note, however, that some words have to be spelt with *-ise* (see the table below). This is because in these cases the endings are not formed from the active suffix but from a larger word element such as *-prise* (meaning 'taking') and *-vise* (meaning 'seeing').

Words spelt with -ise not -ize

advertise	despise	improvise
advise	devise	incise
apprise	dis(en)franchise	merchandise
arise	disguise	prise (open)
chastise	enfranchise	revise
circumcise	enterprise	supervise
comprise	excise	surmise
compromise	exercise	surprise
demise	franchise	televise

jargon

All special spheres of activity develop a special vocabulary – called jargon – used for internal communication: law, medicine, sociology, and (most recently) computing are well-known examples. Other domains, such as journalism, use special words and idioms that are not normally found in general use: *probe* for *investigation* or *investigate*, *quiz* for *interrogate*, *package* for *deal*, and *swap* for *transplant* (in the medical sense). These are typically short words that make for concise expression in newspaper headlines. Problems arise when members of the professions need to communicate with the public at large; then, jargon can easily become gobbledegook. Plain English, i.e. English that everyone can understand, should be clear as well as accurate, and there are dangers when you are writing for a general audience about specialist areas of knowledge or information. In these circumstances it is important to avoid obfuscating language typified by the use of words such as *aforesaid*, *in the event of*, *thereto*, *pursuant to*, and *incumbent on*, as well as technical jargon unfamiliar to the ordinary reader.

join together

The opinion that *join* used with *together* is poor style is a total superstition. English is full of such apparent pleonasms and it is entirely idiomatic:

*Outraged parents **joined together** and surrounded the intruder.*
*Early Punk clothing mixed up every youth style since the war and **joined** them **together** with safety pins*

judicial, judicious

Judicial is the plainer word meaning 'relating to or involving the law or legal judgement' (as in *judicial proceedings*, *a judicial separation*, etc.). *Judicious* has to do with judgement in another sense: it means 'exercising or involving good judgement', i.e. showing wisdom, and is applied to people and their decisions and actions (*a judicious assessment of the problems / a judicious mixture of bribes and promises*).

junction, juncture

These words are confused more often than one might expect, usually *junction* for *juncture*. *Junction* is the act or place of joining: physically it is an intersection of roads or railway lines. *Juncture* can also mean 'a place of joining' but is more commonly used in the sense 'a particular moment in time' (*we are at a critical juncture / at this juncture the guests arrived*).

kind

Of its kind is often used redundantly, as apparently in the following sentence:

*This committee set about establishing a small residential home for old people, the second **of its kind** in the country.*

Here, the kind of home in question has already been identified as 'residential' and 'for old people', and it is unlikely that there is any further qualification to be made to distinguish one 'kind' from another. Therefore, the sentence can conclude . . . *the second in the country*.

kind of, sort of

When *kind of* is preceded by *a* or *the*, which are invariable, usage is straightforward:

a kind of thing
the kind(s) of thing(s) we like
the best sort(s) of thing(s)

Kind and *sort* can be singular or (with *the*, though obviously not with *a*) plural, and the noun following *of* can also be singular or (again with *the kind of* or *the sort of* but not *a sort of*) plural in several combinations.

The difficulties begin with determiners that change in the plural: *this, that, these,* and *those.* (Note that the issues raised here are less common in the case of the third alternative, *type of*.)

When followed by a singular noun, the correct form is *this kind* [or *sort*] *of thing*, not *this kind* [or *sort*] *of a thing*.

When it is followed by a plural noun, many purists insist on making *kind* or *sort* plural as well:

these kinds [or *sorts*] *of things*

The alternative *this kind* [or *sort*] *of things* is ungrammatical, but an alternative style has been in use for several centuries:

these kind [or *sort*] *of things*

This too is technically ungrammatical, but it can be justified if we regard *kind of* as an adjectival phrase qualifying the following noun (*things*), with the demonstrative pronoun *these* or *those* also qualifying *things* rather than *kind* (or *sort*). This solution is well established informally and it is futile to complain about it:

*A lot of players go through **these kind of** rough spells.*
*She knew **these sort of** bargains do crop up from time to time.*

However, for impeccable grammar two other approaches are possible, the one considered above, and another that is based on lateral grammatical thinking:

these kinds (or *sorts*) *of thing(s)*
things of this kind (or *sort*)

*Children like **these kinds of** silly jokes.* (plural noun after *of*)
***These sorts of** incident are particularly disliked by police officers.* (singular noun after *of*)

*Films **of this sort** show directors giving up the attempt to address contemporary anxieties.*

latter

See FORMER *AND* LATTER.

lay, lie

These little verbs cause great trouble because they are related in meaning and the forms themselves overlap: for example, *lay* is the present tense of one verb and the past tense of the other. The most common errors that arise with them are use of *lay* where *lie* is needed and of *laid* where *lain* is needed. The phrasal verbs formed from these verbs (*lay down, lie down, lay off, lay out, lay up, lie up,* etc.) can be especially confusing. The table below should help clarify which is which of these verbs (particular trouble spots are shown with a ✗):

lay is transitive (takes an object: *to lay an egg, to lay your head down*)

present	**lay**	*Lay* the vinyl in place with a surplus curling up the wall.
		They confiscated everything they could *lay* their hands on, even the bed he was lying on.
past	**laid**	The embalmers *laid* him flat on a long wooden table.

As Lisa **laid** (✗ lay) down the phone her hand was shaking.

present participle	**laying**	The queen mates with a winged male and spends her whole life **laying** eggs.
		These organizations protect their subscribers by **laying down** high standards.
past participle (used with *be*, *have*, *has*, etc.)	**laid**	Track could **be laid** only during the warm summer months.
		He bent down and picked up a carrier that he **had laid** on the floor.
		The pots **had been laid out** on the floor upside down.
		The company **has not laid off** any employees.

lie is intransitive (has no object: *to lie on the bed*)

present	**lie**	Another time he got us to **lie** on the floor with our legs in the air.
		The reponsibility **lies** with all of us.
past	**lay**	He **lay** on his back looking up at the cloudless sky.
		In these early years his preferences **lay** elsewhere.
present participle	**lying**	She was aware of **lying** (✗ laying) flat on something soft.

Fortunately no journalists or television crews ***were lying*** (✘ laying) in wait.

past participle **lain** (used with *be, have, has*, etc.)		My passport was wet and creased from where I ***had lain*** (✘ laid) on it all night.

For a moment she ***had lain*** (✘ laid) stunned.

The responsibility ***had lain*** (✘ laid) so heavily that it took some time to readjust.

Zebo ***had*** simply ***lain down*** (✘ laid down) and gone to sleep.

Finally, in order to complete the picture, here are the parts of the other verb *lie*, meaning 'to be untruthful':

present	**lie**	One could not tell the child to ***lie*** to its mother.
past	**lied**	You ***lied*** about being able to sail.
present participle	**lying**	Why ***was*** this man ***lying*** to her?
past participle	**lied**	She went to prison as a suffragette, ***having lied*** about her age and enrolled as a militant.

lead, led

The past tense and past participle of the verb *lead* are both *led* (*things that led them astray* / *has lectured and led workshops*). A common error is to use *lead*, especially for the past tense, possibly by confusion with *read*, which as a past form and past participle is pronounced the same way as *led*.

legendary

Legendary, unlike *mythical*, means much more than 'belonging to legend (or myth)': it evokes an atmosphere of romance:

*Many tales arose out of this **legendary** mountain.*

It is therefore best to keep *legendary* in reserve for people and achievements that belong to the past or are strongly associated with it, where legend is rooted, and to avoid using it in contemporary or definite historical contexts, especially when these are fixed and dated, a circumstance that runs completely counter to legend:

? *A holiday brochure that is also a history lesson in itself is a good briefing for a unique range of military tours that takes in some of the world's **legendary** [✓ famous or historic] battlefields.*

? *Teddy Edwards is one of the **legendary** [✓ great or celebrated] figures of the jazz saxophone.*

? *Keep up your strength for Berlin's **legendary** [✓ renowned or celebrated] nightlife.*

These uses have become popular since the extension of the parent word *legend* to refer to contemporary celebrities such as film stars and pop 'idols'. We cannot say they are wrong, but they devalue or even trivialize a powerful word.

When it is used in contexts that are explicitly historical in nature, the effect is incongruous or even absurd:

✗ *Cromwell for a while dreamed of joining with Queen Christina, daughter of the **legendary** Protestant hero Gustavus Adolphus, in a religious crusade against popery.*

✗ *Depiction of the **legendary** coronation of Charles in Jerusalem, an example of religiously inspired fiction which also appears in the Chroniques de Charlemagne.*

(In both these examples *legendary* is used of a person or event that is historical.)

The effect is however less incongruous when *legendary* is used in predicative position (i.e. after a verb), perhaps because the transfer of meaning from the realm of actual legend is more obvious:

*Mordkovitch is a fantastic fiddler – her Shostakovich recordings are **legendary**.*

less *and* fewer

The reason that choice between *less* and *fewer* causes such angst (more than almost any other topic, except perhaps the split infinitive) is that the often stated basic rule won't take us all the way. It is one of those cases where usage operates on sense, which can override the normal procedures of grammatical agreement (see NONE for another case). What makes it worse is that dogmatic insistence on a principle leads to further confusion and can produce absurdities. Do we want to speak and write sanitized English or idiomatic English?

The problem centres on an erroneous (or supposedly erroneous) use of _less_ where _fewer_ is needed: the problem does not exist in reverse. Typical uses are in attributive position before nouns, _less / fewer_ followed by _than_, and _or less / fewer_ after a noun. The 'rule' is that _fewer_ is used with plural nouns and indicates number (_fewer trains, fewer people_), whereas _less_ is used with singular nouns and indicates amount (_less work, less sugar_). It is generally incorrect to use _less_ with plurals of this kind: _less trains, less people_, although such uses are often heard informally.

However, the sense plays an important role: when the noun denotes an amount or measure rather than a numerical quantity, even if it is in the plural, _less_ is the more natural and idiomatic choice:

It was a cube, **less than** three metres on each side.
Contracts are for periods of not **less than** five years.
**Less than** fifty teachers responded to the questionnaire.
Write fifteen words **or less** to a sentence.

In the last two examples, _fewer_ would emphasize the numerical status of the people or things involved, whereas _less_ emphasizes the overall amount. _Write fifteen words or fewer_ would convey the wrong sense and would be quite unidiomatic.

Note that when _less_ is followed by a noun with an intervening adjective ambiguity can result:

? _There is a need for **less** ambiguous information._

Here, _less_ is correct whether it applies to _ambiguous_ or to _information_, but there is ambiguity: does the sentence mean that the amount of ambiguous information should be reduced (i.e. 'less ambiguous-information'), or that the information overall should be less ambiguous (i.e. 'less-ambiguous information')? The sentence needs to be recast in either of two ways, depending on the meaning intended:

✓ *There is a need for information that is **less** ambiguous.*
or
✓ *There is **less** need for ambiguous information.*

(Note that this problem is not peculiar to *less*: it applies to *more* as well.)

lesser

Lesser is a so-called 'double comparative' formed on *less*, which is itself a comparative. *Lesser* means 'less great or significant' and is typically preceded by a determiner such as *a, the, this, these*, and so on:

*One of the **lesser** joys of management is telling guys they are not in the squad.*
*The accused agreed to plead guilty to a **lesser** charge.*

It should not be used to denote smaller size or amount; in this case use *less* or *smaller* or *lower*:

✗ *As in all industries, for every high paid job there are a multitude of lesser [✓ lower or less well] paid ones.*

liable

See APT, LIABLE, PRONE.

licence, license

In BrE, *licence* is a noun (*a driving licence / the licence fee*) and the corresponding verb is *license* (*to license a vehicle*); the adjectival form is *licensed* (as in *licensed premises*). In AmE the noun and verb have the same form *license*.

lie

See LAY, LIE.

lightening, lightning

Lightening is the present participle of the verb *lighten* meaning 'to make light or lighter' (in both senses, weight and brightness: *the lightening of burdens / colours that need lightening*), whereas *lightning* (without an *e*) is the electrical discharge in a thunderstorm.

like

Like has two controversial uses: one widely disliked and the other widely deplored.

The first is its use as a conjunction. *Like* is a preposition in the sentence *She smiles **like** her sister* and is a conjunction in the sentence *She smiles **like** her sister does*, where it introduces a clause with a verb (*does*). The first is straightforward and uncontroversial but the second is widely disliked and should be avoided. You can use *as* (or *as if* or *as though*) instead:

✗ *Like* (✓ *As*) *I say, he was past his best.*
✗ *It's starting to feel* **like** (✓ *as if*) *we're in injury time.*
✗ *It was meant to look* **like** (✓ *as though*) *they'd been shot in the heart.*

The second controversial use is the informal one commonly heard in youth speech, in which *like* is a kind of meaningless filler (it is technically an adverb here):

✗ *He said* **like** *it was all a load of rubbish.*

like, such as

When *like* is used as a preposition in the sense 'such as', it is not always obvious whether the person or thing specified is included in what follows:

We all need to read more novels **like** *the one under discussion.* (Is the one being discussed included or merely used for comparison?)

Usually *like* is intended to be inclusive (as it probably is in the sentence just given), and the context often removes doubt, but it is sometimes better, in less clear-cut contexts, to avoid ambiguity by using *such as*, which invariably includes and defines, as it would if we recast this sentence in the form:

We all need to read more novels **such as** *the one under discussion.*

liqueur, liquor

Liquor is a word for any alcoholic drink. It is more common in AmE than in BrE, where it has a ring of commercialese. *Liqueur* is a specific kind of alcoholic drink, typically a strong sweet-flavoured drink based on spirits and drunk after a meal.

literally

We need to get a straightforward and uncontroversial use of *literally* out of the way first. Its innocent meaning 'in a literal sense' with reference to words and terminology causes no problems:

*Swastika, a Sanskrit word, means **literally** 'well being'.*

The problems start when *literally* is used as an intensifying word in the context of idiom and metaphor. In this usage it appears to be given a sense contrary to its proper meaning:

*The city felt **literally** soaked in history.*

Obviously, the city was figuratively and not literally soaked in history: if you take *literally* literally that is. This is not a modern linguistic device, however. 'Good' writers, such as the ones below, were using *literally* in this way even in the high period of English literature of the later eighteenth and nineteenth centuries.

Every day with me is literally another yesterday for it is exactly the same.

Alexander Pope, in a letter of 1708

> *Mr Podsnap stood with his back to the drawing-room*
> *fire, pulling up his shirt-collar, like a veritable cock of*
> *the walk literally pluming himself in the midst of his*
> *possessions.*
>
> Charles Dickens, Our Mutual Friend, 1865

One is not of course literally *soaked in history* nor does one *plume oneself* or do any of those odd things that enliven English idiom. What we have here is one figure of speech inside another, and it would be pedantic to object in principle to this kind of light-hearted emphasis; the important point is to avoid a comic effect (which *literally* can undoubtedly have) when you are intending to be serious or at least neutral in tone:

*He had a passion for reading and **literally** devoured any piece of paper that came his way.*
*I went back to the Isle of Man with my tail quite **literally** between my legs.*

Sometimes, *literally* serves to reinforce the appropriateness to a particular situation of the image contained in a metaphor, and in these cases it is appropriate:

*They couldn't cope with the dog and, in desperation, **literally** dumped it on the doorstep.*
*Peter had, **literally**, stumbled on the mouth of the hole.*
*I have had patients who have **literally** laughed out loud and ended up cracking a rib.*
*It was the end of the swinging Sixties and everyone was **literally** having a ball.*

Literally can also be effective in pointing up an idiom that is especially relevant in a particular context, usually involving a play on the words of the metaphor underlying the idiom. But it can become forced and tedious, as often in newspaper reporting, rather like the obligatory punning headlines you find there:

? *The roof **literally** fell in on Montreal last year when storms ripped off their Olympic stadium's retractable top.*
? *Silting of shallow valleys and estuaries has left them almost **literally** high and dry.*
? *The bungalow is **literally** standing in the path of progress.*
? *His teeth had been **literally** knocked down his throat.*
? *It is the glider pilot who **literally** has the life of the tow pilot in his hands.*

It is also poor style to use *literally* in contexts that do not involve metaphor at all, forming a redundant reinforcing tag ('I'm not kidding you'):

? *At the end of parenting women can spend **literally** years in a state of near exhaustion.*
? *The Prime Minister had **literally** no idea that he lacked the means to do what he wanted.*
? *As soon as my name was read out there was that feeling of ecstasy, but **literally** within seconds it turned to nerves.*

loan

Loan is the standard word for a noun in the sense 'something lent or available to be lent'. In the nineteenth century, it was also used as a verb, an alternative to *lend*, and it has continued in use in this sense in AmE and other varieties apart from British:

*Delaney told him he could **loan** him $50 a week.*

It is used in BrE too when the subject is something valuable (such as a work of art) being made available by a formal arrangement to an institution for a period:

*Sir Denis **has loaned** a second Guercino painting to the Gallery.*
*The children examine original documents **loaned** from the local library.*

An alternative to the passive form in the second example, which some prefer, is *on loan* (from).

In general senses, however, *loan* has fallen out of use as a verb in BrE; there are signs of a revival but it is still regarded as poor style as a needless variant of *lend*.

loath, loathe

Loath is an adjective and is pronounced like *both*; it is typically used with *to* in the sense 'reluctant to do something' (*was loath to put his sketches on public display*). *Loathe* (pronounced like *clothe*) is a verb meaning 'to dislike intensely' (*always loathed the idea of white weddings*).

logically

Beware of using *logically* in contexts that have little to do with logic, especially as a sentence adverb qualifying the whole of a statement:

✗ ***Logically**, there is no reason why Bristol City's existence for the past 27 years should have fluctuated between the lower divisions of English football.*

Logic implies argument behind reason, not simply the existence (or absence) of a reason.

loose, lose

It is possible to confuse the spelling of these words in rapid writing. *Loose* is an adjective meaning 'not tight' (also in figurative meanings as in *a loose translation*); as a verb, it means 'to make loose or less tight' and its inflections are *loosing, loosed* (*loosed her sash, sending it snaking to the floor*). It is also used in the context of firing weapons (*loosed a couple of shots at the roof*). An alternative word, except in this last sense, is *loosen*.

Lose means 'to have no longer something one needs' (with related idiomatic meanings) and its inflections are *losing, lost* (*no time to lose / were losing their way in the dark*).

luxuriant, luxurious

Both words are related to the word *luxury*, which is in turn derived from Latin *luxus* meaning 'abundance'. They have overlapped in use since the seventeenth century, but their meanings are distinct. *Luxurious*, the more general word, means 'rich in luxuries or comforts' (*a luxurious villa / kept in the luxurious style they were used to*) whereas *luxuriant* is no longer strongly associated with the notion of luxury but has the specific meaning to do with growth, 'rich or abundant in foliage or vegetation'; it can also be used figuratively (*had blue eyes and a luxuriant curling moustache*).

magic, magical

The two words overlap in the main meanings, 'relating to magic', 'produced by or as if by magic', and 'wonderful', but *magic* and not *magical* is used in certain set terms such as *magic lantern* and *magic square*.

Otherwise *magic* and *magical* are largely interchangeable, but *magical* typically has stronger overtones of wonder and excitement only figuratively related to the notion of magic. So a *magic show* is one in which a conjuror performs tricks, whereas a *magical show* could be any kind of show that is exciting and enjoyable. In recent usage, *magic* has come to be used informally both in attributive position (before a noun) in a similar sense (*had a magic time*), but this is nonstandard and largely associated with the language of children.

majority of

The noun phrase *the majority of* should normally refer to countable items (persons or things) and be followed by a plural noun. When it is the subject of a verb this should also be plural:

*The **majority** of entrants are school-leavers from the UK.*
*The vast **majority** of flights do depart on time.*

Uses with singular nouns are unidiomatic except with collective nouns such as *group, population, public,* etc. which refer effectively to a number of individuals. Any verb of which *majority* is the subject should still be plural:

✓ A **majority** of the population are either totally or partially dependent on public transport.

✗ Leeds had the **majority** of [✓ most of] the play but looked weak in defence.

✗ The **majority** of the housing [✓ most of or nearly all the housing] is in local authority estates with little provision for single people.

✗ The **majority** of the audience was [✓ were] less interested in salving their fears about wars and conflicts ahead.

See also BULK OF.

masterful, masterly

Both words used to share the same meanings derived from various senses of *master*, but in more recent usage they have acquired an important distinction: *masterful* has to do with dominance and power (as with political masters), whereas *masterly* connotes skill and fine qualities (as with artistic masters):

*It was a kind face, but it had a rather **masterful** look about it. The broad comedy he brings into the drama is performed with **masterly** finesse.*

When there is a wrong choice, *masterful* tends to be used for *masterly* rather than the other way round:

✗ That Gregory was a **masterful** storyteller has long been recognized.

✗ Veblen's achievement was to capture the strategies of the leisure class in a series of classic phrases and categories and exemplify them clearly and in detail with a **masterful** sense of irony.

The adverb *masterfully* occasionally occurs doubling erroneously as an adverb for *masterly*, which lacks a single-word equivalent:

✗ *For over twenty years, Hugo had **masterfully** deployed the metaphor of the wave.*

It is important to respect the distinction in meaning since the contexts are often such that ambiguity can arise.

may

See CAN, MAY.

maybe, may be

There is a difference in spelling between the adverb *maybe* (= 'perhaps', one word) and the verbs *may be* (two words) used compositionally with each having its full meaning:

Maybe *I would have been offered a discount if I had brought my wife too.*
*It **may be** that I would have been offered a discount if I had brought my wife too.*

As a rule of thumb, see if you can substitute *could* for *may*. If you can (as in the second sentence above but not the first), then *may* is a separate word and must be spelt that way.

media

Media, in its meaning 'the organs of public news communication', is in origin a plural form of the singular noun *medium*. But because *medium* is hardly ever used in this meaning, *media* has encroached on it grammatically and become in effect a singular mass noun, like *data*. For this reason it is often used with singular verbs and determiners (*this* and *that* instead of *these* and *those*, and so on):

? The **media** has [✓ have] been subjected to a barrage of restrictive legislation.

? The British **media** at its [✓ their] finest is [✓ are] the best in the world.

? The principal agency at this level is the mass **media** in all its [✓ their] forms: books, magazines, newspapers, cinema, theatre, and television.

There is still some opposition to this development, because unlike the more amalgamated notion of *data*, *media* still implies a range of separate and identifiable elements (the press, radio, television, and so on). In time *media* may well go the way of *data*, but in the meantime it is advisable to regard *media* as a plural noun: this is never wrong and it often makes better sense (as well as better grammar):

✓ The **media** have decided that there has been a return to two-party politics.

✓ We can identify pressures which serve to disable the **media** from meeting their own criteria of objectivity.

meet with

Use of *meet with* in the sense of encountering a person or people (*met with her opposite number in the White House*) is typical of AmE and is increasingly used in BrE too, although it is often disapproved of in Britain because *meet* is considered adequate by itself. In BrE, however, one *meets with* some kind of experience or reaction, usually unfortunate or unwelcome, or at least unexpected:

*Generally speaking, family planning in San Salvador **has met with** a hostile reception.*
*When the Prime Minister tried to share a toast with his adoptive mother, he **was met with** an uncomprehending stare.*

mendacity, mendicity

Mendacity is derived from Latin *mendax* meaning 'false'; it means 'a tendency to be untruthful'. *Mendicity*, on the other hand, is more honourable: it is based on Latin *mendicare* meaning 'to beg' and means 'begging' (compare *mendicant* in *mendicant friar*, a friar who lived off alms).

meretricious, meritorious

Here is another pair of words that are confused because they are not often used, causing doubts about them. *Meretricious* is derived from the Latin word *meretrix* meaning 'prostitute' and it means 'speciously showy, tawdry'. It is important not to use this word in error when you mean *meritorious*, which (as its form suggests) means 'deserving merit'.

The captain's citation commended him for 'exceptionally **meritorious** *conduct in the performance of outstanding service'.*

What worried him most, apart from the **meretricious** *glitter of the whole charade, was the erosion of the proper role of Cabinet Ministers.*

misnomer

A *misnomer* is the wrong use of a name for something or someone inappropriate or undeserving, as in Byron's comment *My name of Epic's no misnomer*. It originated as a legal word meaning 'a mistake in naming a person or thing' and was often used as a 'non-count' noun like *fraud*. In time it came to mean 'the use of a wrong name' in any context, which is the meaning current today:

In truth, the Social Democratic and Labour Party has long been a **misnomer**. *Much of the working-class element drifted off long ago.*

What a *misnomer* is not is a word or description wrongly chosen in a particular context:

✗ *It would be a* **misnomer** *to say Conan Doyle 'concentrated' on his writing in this period.*
✗ *Kirkby was partly made as a result of an overflow from Liverpool, so it's a* **misnomer** *to say it's not in Liverpool just because it is over a line.*

In these examples, there is no question of a name being wrongly applied, but of a wrong word or phrase being chosen, and in the second example it is not even a question of a word or name, but of an assertion. The better word in these cases is *misconception* or even just *mistake*.

misuse

See ABUSE, MISUSE.

mitigate, militate

That night, there was little to **mitigate** *his depression.*
Justice requires the handing over of these people, but expediency, I fear, **militates** *against it.*

These words are often confused because they have a similar sound and rhythm, and both have meanings to do with reducing or preventing things. *Mitigate* is a transitive verb (i.e. it takes an object) and means 'to reduce the harm or severity of', whereas *militate* is intransitive, is followed by *against*, and means 'to counteract, to have a beneficial effect against'.

Take care to avoid using *mitigate* with *against*: in the first example below *mitigate* is correct but *against* is not, while in the second example *mitigate* is the wrong choice altogether and *militate* is the correct one:

✗ *It is possible to* **mitigate against** [✓ *mitigate* or *lessen* or *reduce*] *any loss by arranging insurance cover.*
✗ *Various factors appear to* **mitigate against** [✓ *militate against* or *prevent* or *inhibit*] *full use of the systems by the teacher.*

mixed metaphor

English, like all languages, uses words in figurative ways, transferring the meaning from one type of context to another. This is known as metaphor, and a word or phrase used in this way is called a metaphor. Metaphor goes beyond comparing one thing with another (this is called a simile) and actually applies the name:

(simile) *The music is like a vast cathedral of sound*.
(metaphor) *The music is a vast cathedral of sound*.

The whole business of metaphor is more fully discussed in *How to Write Better English*, pp. 169–71; here we are concerned with the trap of using metaphors that clash, so-called 'mixed' metaphors, in the same sentence or passage. Sometimes one is not even aware that what one has said is in fact a metaphor, because language is so full of them. Mixed metaphors are not 'wrong' in the sense of being ungrammatical but they can be distracting and the effect can often be comic or absurd:

The flood of offers sparked speculation in other stocks.
(A flood cannot produce sparks.)
The campaign was intended to trumpet the retailer's ethical milestones.
(Trumpeting is a musical celebration, not done at milestones.)
A North London council has helped fuel the anti-Tesco backlash.
(A backlash is a violent backward movement that is not dependent on fuel.)
It becomes clear that it is a deliberately dud piece of legislation with more loopholes than a rollercoaster.

(A loophole was originally a small hole in a defensive wall, for firing guns through. The writer may have been thinking of loops in the rollercoaster's track.)

Some idioms are mini-metaphors that can sound incongruous or counterintuitive when they occur together:

A new version of the program has appeared – hopefully with all the bugs ironed out.

This does not mean that we have constantly to micromanage figurative uses, which would bring ordinary discourse to a halt. Language is permeated with figurative meanings that have a life of their own and cannot be made to conform too rigidly to their physical counterparts. There is nothing wrong with *increasing targets* (= 'objectives'), even though strictly speaking a physical target is easier to reach when larger; nor with *reducing ceilings* (= 'limits, especially on spending') although this is an impossibility in the literal sense.

momentarily

Usage of this word differs between British and American usage. To begin with, the pronunciations vary: in British English the stress is on the first syllable (*mo-ment-*) and in American English it is on the third (*-ar-i-ly*).

More importantly, there is a difference in the range of meanings. In both British and American usage *momentarily* means 'for a moment' or 'briefly':

*He looked **momentarily** startled, then smiled at them both.*

*It was a magical feeling to possess, **momentarily**, such a beautiful, wild creature.*

*Such culinary and aesthetic delights will create the illusion, albeit **momentarily**, that your garden is within earshot of the Mediterranean's balmy shores.*

In American usage it has an additional and more common meaning 'at any moment, very shortly':

*The doctor came over **momentarily**.*

*The operation will begin **momentarily**.*

This meaning is creeping into British use, and the word is best avoided in contexts that might be ambiguous.

much

See VERY, MUCH.

mutual, common

> *They parted at last with mutual civility, and possibly a mutual desire of never meeting again.*
>
> Jane Austen, *Pride and Prejudice*, 1813

The traditional view about the use of these words is that *common* denotes sharing between a number of people or things (as in *speaking a common language*) whereas *mutual* implies reciprocal feelings or actions (as in *mutual love* and *mutual congratulation*). In practice, however, the distinction is not always clear-cut, and both words tend to draw their meanings from the contexts in which they are used:

*Without friendship and **mutual** confidence, without the ability to speak to one another candidly and lovingly, we shall never be in a position where our relationship can change things.*

*The Prime Minister softened the announcement that he would quit within a year by joking that his last TUC speech would be 'to the **mutual** relief of both of us'.*

*Their tactics were so successful that within a year both husbands were allowed to return home. When their **mutual** boss discovered this coincidence she urged them to write a book describing how they applied their boardroom skills to managing their husbands.*

Reciprocity is explicit in the first example and implicit in the second and third; it would be absurd to allow one but not the others on this ground alone. *Mutual* is also usually the only choice when it is predicative in position (i.e. after a verb), since *common* in this position invariably means 'frequent' (and would make no sense in sentences such as the one below):

*I thought her the most beautiful thing I'd ever seen and, amazingly, the attraction was **mutual**.*

But where the notion is primarily of sharing (typically with words such as *interests, objectives, purpose, values,* etc.) and only remotely of interaction, *common* is often preferable:

*The hub of the new relationship with Russia has to be a recognition of **common** values.*

*He called for all communities to pull together as part of a **common** purpose and **common** effort.*

*Individuals with a **common** interest, for example engineers, post open messages to other authorized members.*

It is useful, in modern English, to distinguish between *mutual consent*, which refers to agreement by (normally two) particular parties, and *common consent*, which is general agreement involving anyone who might take an interest. But not all nineteenth-century writers saw it in this way (see below).

> *The dull life in the square-built house was only relieved now and then by a stiff dinner party, at which a few country people assembled to bore each other by mutual consent.*

Mary Braddon, Lady Audley's Secret, 1862

HISTORICAL NOTE – Nineteenth-century grammarians, with Latin grammar very much at the back of their minds, decided that *mutual* should mean more than just 'shared', a meaning it had had for three centuries already and which it has in Dickens's title *Our Mutual Friend* (1865). But the rule has always been undermined by the plurality of meaning inherent in the proposed alternative *common*, and in particular by its meaning 'vulgar, lacking refinement' which makes *a common friend* potentially ambiguous, although in current English this ambiguity is more theoretical than actual because this sense of *common* is in decline. It is, however, useful to have the distinction between *mutual friends* (= friends of each other) and *common friends* (= friends shared by another).

names *and* proper nouns

Names of people and places are called *proper nouns* because they are 'proper' (in the old meaning of 'belonging specially') to a particular person or thing. They are normally spelt with a capital initial letter. Some personal names are spelt in different ways (e.g. *Ann / Anne*; *Catherine / Katharine / Katherine*; *Jonathan / Jonathon / Jonothan*). The same applies to some surnames (e.g. *Allan / Allen*; *Macdonald / McDonald*; *Ramsay / Ramsey*). Take care to use the right form for the person you are naming or addressing.

Here is a list of some names that are often misspelt:

Afghanistan
Buddha
Colombia (in S. America)
Columbia (in Canada, and District of Columbia in Washington DC)
Copenhagen
Dostoevsky
Frances (female personal name)
Francis (male personal name, also used as a surname)
Gandhi
Gloucester
Grieg
Guatemala
Guinevere (wife of King Arthur)
Gwynedd (in Wales)
Housman (English poet)
Huguenot
Luxembourg
Massachusetts

Mediterranean
Michelangelo
Mississippi
Muhammad
Neanderthal
Niagara
Nietzsche
Nuremberg
Nureyev
Philip (but the surname is usually Phillips)
Piccadilly
Pyrenees
Rembrandt
Romania
Roosevelt
Scheherazade
Shakespeare
Sidney (personal name)
Solzhenitsyn
Strasbourg
Sydney (in Australia)
Worcester

need

See DARE, NEED.

negatives

For ambiguity when *because* is used with a negative, see BECAUSE.

neither

See EITHER, NEITHER.

none

None is a pronoun that stands for *not one* or *not any* (*none of the people present / none of the information*). It is a superstition that *none* must always be followed by a singular verb; the grammar depends on the sense implied:

None of the faults so far reported is due to this cause. (Emphasizes individuals: *not one*.)
None of the faults so far reported are due to this cause. (Emphasizes the group as a whole: *not any.*)

In this respect *none* behaves in the same way as *no*, which can also go with singular or plural forms (*no money, no house, no shoes, no crowds*).

When the emphasis is on a single person or thing, the verb is singular:

*She said it all, knowing full well that **none** of it **was** heard.*
None of the rooms is suitable.
None of the partners here is actually entitled to a salary.

When the main idea is of several people or things considered together, or an indefinite number, the verb can be plural:

*Why do **none** of the children distinguish between 'its' and 'it's'?*
*Standards slipped but there were **none** of the old crowd now to witness the decay.*

*Special Branch keeps records on many millions of people **none**
of whom **have** committed any offence.*
***None** of the musicians look or sound as if they are enjoying the
experience.*

(In the last example, using singular verbs *looks* and
sounds would involve a problem of gender-neutrality
in the continuation of the sentence: *he or she* would be
clumsy, and gender-neutral *they* would highlight the
awkwardness with *none*.)

> *The air was filled with phantoms, wandering hither
> and thither in restless haste, and moaning as they went.
> Every one of them wore chains like Marley's Ghost;
> some few (they might be guilty governments) were
> linked together; none were free.*
>
> Charles Dickens, *A Christmas Carol*, 1843

number of

See AMOUNT OF, NUMBER OF.

observance, observation

Observance is the normal choice in meanings to do
with respecting laws and rules and carrying out duties
and formal procedures, whereas *observation* is used in
more physical senses to do with seeing and perceiving,
and has the special meaning 'a remark or comment'
(*several astute observations*). It is used in special combinations such as *observation car* (on a train, chiefly
AmE) and (in military contexts) *observation post*.

of *in* must of, should of, *etc.*

✗ *Somebody **must of** [✓ must have] put it there.*
✗ *We **should of** [✓ should have] got some more to drink.*

Using *of* instead of *have* after *must*, *should*, *would*, and
other auxiliary verbs, which arises from the similarity
of sound in rapid speech, is regarded as illiterate. Its
use in print should be avoided at all costs.

See also BORED.

official, officious

As an adjective, *official* means 'relating to a job or
office' (*official duties*) and 'authorized or confirmed by
authority' (*the official attendance figures*).

Officious is an evaluating word meaning 'asserting
authority aggressively or intrusively', and is typically
applied to the exercise of authority:

*He heard the sound of **officious** voices calling to the driver to
stop.*
*It was not merely **officious** but often dangerous to move a
drunk from the place he had chosen to lie down into one where
he had not.*

one

In the phrase *one of those* (or *the people, etc.*) *who . . .*,
it is preferable to follow it with a plural verb (agreeing
with *those* rather than *one*), except when emphasis is

needed on the individuality of *one*, in which case a singular verb is used:

(plural) *She was **one of those women** who never **give** anybody the satisfaction of her undivided attention.*
(singular) *The Meeting House is **one of those places** which **is** open to the general public on Sundays for religious worship.*

A plural construction is especially useful when there is a mix of grammatical person (first and third person in the following sentence):

*I'm **one of the few people** who **have** actually got the guts now to stand up and say that.*

The use of *one* to mean 'any person', 'I', or 'me' can seem to be an affectation, especially when it is closely associated with the speaker or writer, but the only convenient alternative is *you* and *your*, which conveys a more casual tone that involves the reader in a way that may not be suitable:

*It was enough to make **your** hair stand on end.*

When the context is generalized and the natural meaning is 'any person' (including only incidentally the speaker), *one* is more idiomatic:

***One** should never speak about things that one does not know.*

USAGE NOTE – When *one* is used in this way BrE and AmE differ with regard to choice of further pronoun having the same reference in a continuation of the sentence. In AmE, *one* is followed either by another *one* (or *one's* or *oneself*) or by a third-person pronoun *he* or *she* (or gender-neutral *they*), by *himself* or *herself*, or by *his* or *her* or *their*, or *themselves*, whereas in BrE another *one* (or *one's* or *oneself*) always follows:

(AmE) I like to believe one can be honest and sincere and committed in what he's doing.
(BrE) One can never quite believe what one sees.

one another

See EACH OTHER, ONE ANOTHER.

ongoing

Despite occasional protests against the need for *ongoing*, it is a word that can be useful in conveying continuation to the present (or to the time being referred to), and is not always satisfactorily replaced by *continuing*, *developing*, and other proposed alternatives:

✓ *There has been a long **ongoing** battle between alternative medical practice and orthodox medicine.*

The key here is discretion. Since *ongoing* jars with many readers as an unattractive neologism, if you suspect that your readers might bridle at it, you can often avoid using it. The alternatives – including rephrasing – can often be just as effective:

? *There is an **ongoing** [✓ constant or current] need for staff training.*

? *If your problem is **ongoing** [✓ If your problem persists], ask your doctor to refer you to a dermatologist.*

? *We have an **ongoing** [✓ continuing] campaign to ensure that marked diesel oil is only used for its intended purpose.*

? *An investigation was **ongoing** [✓ in progress] but she hoped an inquest would open very soon.*

only

For the position of *only* in a sentence, see ADVERBS, *position of adverbs*.

on to, onto

On to is what is known as a 'complex preposition', a preposition made up of several words (like *out of* and *up to*). It has been around since the sixteenth century, and a one-word form *onto* has existed from the seventeenth century. Both forms are used in current English, but *onto* has not been as widely accepted as *into*, which dates from Old English:

*Louise flopped **on to** the sofa.*
*Do not throw rubbish **onto** an open fire in the living room.*

Note that in some uses *on* retains its separate meaning and needs to be written separately: *the pilot flew onto an airstrip further south* means that he landed on it, whereas *the pilot flew on to an airstrip further south* (with *on* belonging with *flew* and *to* with the rest of the sentence) means that he flew in that direction: the aircraft is on the ground in the first version and still in the air in the second.

Care also needs to be taken to preserve the identity of *on* in phrasal verbs when these are followed by *to*:

*It was a while before I **latched on** | to what she was asking.*

When *to* is part of a to-infinitive it obviously cannot be joined to a preceding *on*:

*Many secretaries **go on** | to become assistant PR executives.*

(Note that in the last two structures the same restriction would apply to *in to*.)

-or

See -ER, -OR.

oral, verbal

An *oral* statement is one that is spoken as distinct from written or printed (or, these days, emailed or texted); a *verbal* statement is one using words as distinct from gestures, pictures, and other forms of communicating information and ideas. A *verbal agreement*, which is an agreement reached by discussion and not written down, should strictly speaking be called an *oral agreement*, but the expression is firmly established and it is futile to object to it.

ordinance, ordnance, ordonnance

An *ordinance* is an order or command, *ordnance* is military stores and materials, and (the much less common) *ordonnance* is an arrangement of parts in art, architecture, and literature. *Ordnance Survey* is the official British organization that produces large-scale regional maps, so called because it was originally administered by the Master of Ordnance.

ought

Ought is an unusual verb which has an important feature and an equally important deficiency:

• it is a modal verb and can form negatives directly with *not*, and questions by simple inversion, without needing the support of *do*:

*An artist, he told her, **ought not** to have to starve.*
***Ought you** to be telling me this?*

• but it has no past form and cannot even form one with *do*. Instead, the tense is expressed by the accompanying verb (*know* in the example below):

*Investors **ought to have known** that a risk was involved.*

It is incorrect to write *did ought*, and *didn't ought*, though more common, is even worse:

✗ *He's only the driver, and **didn't ought** [✓ ought not] to be there.*

ours

There is no apostrophe: *this work of ours.*

overestimate, underestimate

Beware of using *underestimate* when you mean *over-estimate*, typically in a negative context such as *such-and-such cannot be overestimated* (i.e. such-and-such is considerable):

✗ *The importance of Shakespeare to the curriculum cannot be underestimated [✓ overestimated].*

owing to

See DUE TO.

oxymoron

The term is derived from two Greek words opposed in meaning, *oxus* meaning 'sharp' and *moros* meaning 'dull'. It is a figure of speech in which two words opposite in meaning are used together for special effect, as in *a cheerful pessimist* and *harmonious discord.* An oxymoron is therefore something intentional or even ingenious; it should not be used (although it often is) to mean an accidental or casual contradiction in terms:

✗ *May I nominate A. D. J. Porter for an award for producing the **oxymoron** of the year – 'an unbiased New Zealander'?*

participles

A participle is a form of a verb ending in *-ing* (the present participle, e.g. *aiming, moving, spending*) or *-ed* / *-t* or *-en* (the past participle, e.g. *cooked, lent, eaten, taken*); some past participles are irregular (e.g. *go, gone* and *make, made*). Participles are used to form certain tenses of verbs (e.g. *they are eating*) and passives (e.g. *the meal was eaten*). They are also used to form subordinate clauses attached to the main clauses of sentences:

Taking the book in her hand, she marched out of the room.
Born in Alberta, he was educated at the universities of Toronto and Chicago.

Normally the participle refers to the subject of the main part of the sentence (*she* and *he* above), and it is important not to misrelate the two parts by making the participle relate to some other word in the sentence (a practice known as a 'dangling' or 'hanging' participle):

✗ *Wearing a woolly kilt and sensible shoes, her programme became popular as she used her forceful techniques to teach dogs obedience.*

The part underlined seems from the grammar to be attached to 'her programme', whereas of course it was the woman herself who wore the kilt and shoes. This can be improved as follows:

✓ *Her programme became popular as, wearing a woolly kilt and* _sensible shoes_, she used her forceful techniques to teach dogs obedience.

✓ _She wore a woolly kilt and sensible shoes, and_ her programme became popular as she used her forceful techniques to teach dogs obedience.

✗ In 1763, _while still **learning** the violin_, his father took the young Wolfgang and his sister on a tour.

It was of course the young Wolfgang who was still learning the violin and not, as the structure of the sentence implies, his father, but this wrong interpretation can only be rejected on the basis of common sense and the reader's knowledge. There are several ways of recasting the sentence to avoid this error:

✓ In 1763, _while the young Wolfgang was still learning the violin_, his father took him and his sister on a tour.

A passive construction is also possible:

✓ In 1763 Wolfgang, _who was still learning the violin_, was taken by his father on a tour with his sister.

partly, partially

These two words are close in meaning – too close for comfort – and the choice can be difficult. A convenient guide is to think of _partly_ as the opposite of _wholly_ or _entirely_, and _partially_ as the opposite of _completely_; then the words tend to fall into place. Compare the following two sentences:

The hillside has been **partly** terraced.
The hillside has been **partially** terraced.

The first version means that the terracing is a feature of part of the hillside (i.e. it is not *wholly* terraced), whereas the second means that the terracing has yet to be finished (i.e. it is not *completely* terraced).

This rule works reasonably well, but *partly* is more common and tends to intrude on the meaning identified for *partially*:

*The two long porticoes have been **partly** excavated and restored.*
*Amalfi Cathedral has been **partly** rebuilt.*
*They want a stake in the **partly** privatized telecommunications organization.*

The following additional notes might be helpful:

• *Partly* works better when it is linked to a verb (especially an active one, as below) or applies to a whole sentence or idea:

*The choice of treatment depends **partly** on the age of the patient.*

• There is the added complication that *partially* has another meaning, the opposite of *impartially*, which can get in the way:

? *He was **partially** excluded* [**?** = 'excluded partly' or 'in a partial, i.e. unfair, way'] *from the competition.*

• *Partly* is generally preferred in contrastive uses where it is repeated or balanced by a corresponding word:

*He was **partly** irritated and **partly** mystified.*

*County clubs were financed **partly** by gate money and **partly** from the subscriptions of members.*
*The analysis employed is based **partly** on party records and private papers but **chiefly** on an extensive range of local newspapers.*

> The statue fell in fragments on the floor. With a
> confused sensation in me, which was partly anger and
> partly distress, I stooped to look at the fragments. When
> I rose again, the Shadow had vanished and I saw no
> more.
>
> Wilkie Collins, *Armadale*, 1866

• Where the meaning is 'up to a point' and an adjective follows, *partially* is the usual choice:

*For any scheme to be **partially** exempt from tax the programme must be open to all employees.*
*You could finish up at least **partially** buried if there was a cave-in.*
*A class of **partially** free serfs are coerced and exploited by a dominant aristocracy of landlords.*
*All hair tonics need to be shaken before use to disperse the essences which are only **partially** soluble in water.*

• *Partially* is also used in certain fixed compounds such as *partially deaf* and *partially sighted*.

passed, past

It is perhaps a little confusing to say that *passed* is the past tense and past participle of the verb *pass* (*we passed by on the other side / poor Jim was passed over*), and should not be mistaken in spelling for *past*, which is a preposition and adverb (*walked past the gate / a van flashed past*), but the examples given should make the point clear. The distinction is also illustrated by comparing *we passed the house* with *we went past the house*.

peaceable, peaceful

In general, *peaceable* means 'disposed to peace, not inclined to dispute or quarrel'; it refers primarily to people or animals or their activities, and the adverb *peaceably* is almost as common:

*Anxiety can turn a normally **peaceable** horse into an angry, rearing, uncontrollable animal when brought near a mare that is in season.*
*I'm a **peaceable** man but I'll murder 'em if they come up here with their bulldozers.*
*Welcome to our **peaceable** kingdom.*
*On the whole they lived **peaceably** and had lots of fellowship together.*

The more common word *peaceful* means 'untroubled by conflict, tranquil'; the notion is more actual than potential and it can describe a person as well as an activity or situation:

*Members should be free to engage in **peaceful** political activity.*
*I'm a quiet **peaceful** person. Do stop being so intense.*
*The siege ended **peacefully**.*

peremptory, perfunctory

Here is another pair of words that can be confused from under-familiarity, since they are not needed very often and their meanings overlap. A *peremptory* order or instruction is one that must be complied with urgently; it does not just mean 'abrupt' or 'curt' although it may be those things as well:

✓ He hated the drudgery of compiling lists to **peremptory** deadlines.

✗ Bruce brushed him aside with a **peremptory** wave of his hand.

Perfunctory means 'routine or mechanical':

The address was greeted with barely five seconds of **perfunctory** applause.

perquisite, prerequisite

A *perquisite* is an extra benefit a person receives in their job or employment; it is usually shortened to *perk*. A *prerequisite* is something required as a condition before something else can be granted or done: *Clear-sightedness is a prerequisite of effective action.*

piteous, pitiable, pitiful

All three words share the basic meaning 'arousing or deserving pity' and are largely interchangeable; *pitiful* is the most common (*there was a pitiful smile on her face*) and *piteous* tends to sound literary (*It came again, a most piteous keening sound*).

The form of *pitiable* emphasizes the notion of actual pity, and both it and *pitiful* can convey the meaning 'evoking mingled pity and contempt':

*She saw him for what he was: a **pitiable** victim of his mother's obsession.*

Only *pitiful* can be used in the meaning 'absurdly small or insignificant':

*Crowe then had the vulgar audacity to offer me a **pitiful** ten quid if I revealed the manager's name.*

Plain English

See JARGON.

pore, pour

The usual word, in the basic sense 'to make liquid flow', is *pour*: *poured some milk / is pouring with rain / the crowds poured out*, and so on. In the meaning 'to study closely', the word is *pore*, which is used with *over*:

*For planning, we spent long weekends **poring** over the maps.*

portentous, pretentious

Note that the spelling of the first word is *-tous* and not *-tious*. It means 'eliciting amazement or wonder' and is never far away from the notion of a portent or warning:

*At a later time there occurred **portentous** earthquakes and floods.*
*The content and practice of both religion and science were differentiated and reassessed in new and **portentous** ways.*

Portentous also means 'self-consciously important or solemn' and in this meaning it shades into meanings that *pretentious* has, especially when applied to people:

*I am one of what must be an increasing number who find the **portentous** moralisings of Solzhenitsyn a bore and an irritation.*

When the sense is markedly unfavourable, and not equivocal as in the last example, the word needed is *pretentious*:

✗ *Their sporadic and tentative remarks amplified by the vacant acoustics into **portentous** [✓ pretentious] gobbledegook.*

practical, practicable

Practical describes what is possible in practice as distinct from theory, and can also refer to a person in the sense 'showing a realistic approach to difficulties' and 'able to perform manual tasks well':

*The book is full of **practical** advice for homeowners.*
*The theoretical approach described in this chapter needs to be supplemented by **practical** experience.*

Practicable means 'able to be carried out, feasible', is more usually applied to a particular instance under consideration, and occurs much less often in attributive position (before a noun):

*The treatment should be continued for as long as is **practicable**.*

See also IMPRACTICAL, IMPRACTICABLE.

practice, practise

In BrE *practice* is the noun (*is still a common practice / less difficult in practice*) and *practise* is the verb (*spent hours practising / Churches that practise this sort of Christianity*). In AmE *practise* is used for both noun and verb.

precipitate, precipitous

A *precipitate* action or remark is one done or made hastily or without much thought:

*We're not really rushing into this, however **precipitate** it might seem on the surface.*

Precipitous means 'dangerously steep or high', usually in the physical contexts of cliffs and heights and so on, but also in figurative uses:

*The election coincided with a **precipitous** slide in the popularity of a Conservative government struggling with a severe balance of payments deficit.*

prescribe, proscribe

These two words tend to be confused, but they have meanings that are practically opposite. *Prescribe* means 'to recommend or authorize':

*It is not possible to **prescribe** a single examination schedule which is appropriate for all products and all situations.*
*Your doctor may also **prescribe** extra vitamins or iron tablets for you.*

To *proscribe* something is to prohibit it formally:

*Fornication, marriage, gambling, and the haunting of taverns or playhouses were strictly **proscribed**.*

So remember that if a book is *prescribed*, it is recommended or put on a syllabus; if it is *proscribed* it is banned. An important difference!

presently

The meaning differs between British and American English, and the American use has begun to impinge on the British. The traditional British meaning is 'in a while, soon' and normally refers to past time:

*I heard Dad going out to a meeting and **presently** Mum appeared with some food.*

The American meaning (which was formerly also used in British English) is 'at present, now', and normally refers to the time of utterance:

*Very little of this information is **presently** available in electronic form.*

The context, and in particular the tense (past, present, or future) of the verb, usually makes it clear which meaning is intended.

> *He prolonged his scrutiny some minutes. Presently he addressed me: 'Your name, little girl?' 'Jane Eyre, sir.'*
>
> Charlotte Brontë, *Jane Eyre*, 1847

presume

See ASSUME, PRESUME.

pretentious

See PORTENTOUS, PRETENTIOUS.

prevaricate, procrastinate

The two words overlap in meaning and can be used in the same sorts of context, and so they are often confused. To *prevaricate* is to speak or act evasively, whereas to *procrastinate* is to put something off or play for time. These two meanings are much too close for comfort:

*He continued to **prevaricate** even as the deadline for registering as a candidate approached.*
*His successors were less committed and **procrastinated** interminably.*

Prevaricate is often the better word where *procrastinate* is used, but it cannot be called wrong because it also fits the sense of the context:

? *Philosophers need to stop **procrastinating** and staring at their navels and answer questions like the one above with a definite answer.*

principal, principle

Even the most hardened writers can get these spellings wrong occasionally. The usual mistake is to use *principle* for *principal* rather than the other way round.

Principal is an adjective and noun and essentially means 'chief' (*the principal reason / the college principal*), whereas *principle* is a noun only and means 'a fundamental law or truth' (*a matter of principle*) or (in the plural) 'rules of conduct' (*moral principles*).

procrastinate

See PREVARICATE, PROCRASTINATE.

prone

See APT, LIABLE, PRONE.

purposely, purposefully

Purposely means 'deliberately or intentionally'. It is equivalent to *on purpose* but is grammatically more mobile in the sentence:

*It wasn't that I was being **purposely** unfriendly.*
*Others, either **purposely** or accidentally, found the war useful to further their careers.*

Purposefully is the adverb from the adjective *purposeful* and means 'with a strong purpose, with determination':

*Dominic was walking softly but **purposefully** along the gallery, coming straight towards her.*

A third word, *purposively*, means 'for a particular purpose', and is more usual in technical contexts:

*Thus the elements of structure have to behave **purposively**, working at and overcoming basic human problems.*

quite

*In the sunshine it would be **quite** warm.*
*All the ships were bulk carriers, and many were **quite** new.*

Quite has two meanings that merge into one another in such a way that the intended meaning is not always clear. Its main meaning in modern usage is 'fairly' or 'somewhat', which is probably what it means in the sentences given above. But *quite* has another meaning, 'fully' or 'completely', as in *have you quite finished*? In some cases the context makes it clear which aspect of *quite* is intended:

*It is **quite** [= completely] true that a polythene liner is capable of lasting for ten years or more.*
*It would be **quite** [= utterly] wrong to base our conclusions solely on submissions made by members of the public.*
*My mother, I'm afraid, went **quite** [= completely] to pieces after his death.*
*Computer parts can be **quite** [= fairly, somewhat] expensive.*

*It was a poor year if he didn't earn six thousand pounds, **quite** a sum* [= a large sum] *for those days.*

(Note the idiomatic use in the last example of *quite a* – followed by a noun, used to express extremes.)

In other cases the intended sense can be unclear:

*The effect of this can be **quite** [? = somewhat or utterly] shocking.*
*A small bag of sand did the job **quite** [? = fairly or very] nicely.*

If using *quite* could cause a possible doubt in your readers – especially in writing when tone of voice is not there to clarify the meaning – it is best to use an alternative word, such as *completely*, *entirely*, *fully*, or *utterly* in the stronger sense and *fairly*, *rather* or *somewhat* in the weaker sense.

When used with a negative word (*not*, *never*, etc.) the meaning is '[not] completely' or '[not] entirely':

*The place was **not quite** the 'honeymoon cottage' it has often been called.*
*She **never quite** knew what to make of Maurice.*

rather than

The phrase *rather than* can mean either (1) 'and not' or 'instead of' or (2) 'in preference to', and this difference in emphasis affects the way it is used. When the contrast is between paired nouns, adjectives, or adverbials, usage is straightforward:

*Such inscriptions were non-existent **rather than** just rare.*
*He was trained in action **rather than** (in) comfort.*

*They seemed playful **rather than** aggressive.*
*As a television viewer his tastes run to Bruckner **rather than** (to) Cilla Black.*
*Liz was humiliated by this, **rather than** enraged.*

Note that you can repeat the linking words (prepositions) *in* and *to* or you can leave them out: there is little difference except that the flow of the sentence is often improved when they are left out.

The problems begin with pronouns, which change their form. Do you say *rather than me* or *rather than I*? The answer is to be guided by the word that comes before *rather*:

*I wanted to tell **her** rather than **him**.*
***She**, rather than **he**, was the person I wanted to see.*

If a noun comes before *rather* and a pronoun is needed after it, you can determine which pronoun to use after it by substituting a pronoun for the noun. For example:

*I was hoping to ask **Anne** rather than **he/him**.*

The pronoun in place of *Anne* would be *her*: and so the following pronoun would be *him*:

*I was hoping to ask **her** rather than **him**.*

So the correct form within the original sentence is:

*I was hoping to ask **Anne** rather than **him**.*

(The same applies to alternatives such as *instead of* or *and not*, which could be used in these sentences in place of *rather than*.)

The choices can be even more confusing when verbs

are involved: do you use an -*ing* form after *rather than* or a simple form of the verb?

*He let them sleep on, **rather than** wake/waking them.*

An -*ing* form is more common when the meaning tends to be 'instead of', i.e. when the second alternative is rejected or did not happen. (The distinction is therefore clearer in sentences that are couched in the past tense.) In the sentence above, *rather than* introduces an action that was rejected and therefore not performed (he did not wake them, he let them sleep on), and so the choice would be:

*He let them sleep on, **rather than** waking them.*

But

*He will let them sleep on **rather than** wake them*

is more typical because – with the choice still looking into the future and with both possibilities still open – the contrast is essentially one of preference.

When the clause with *rather than* comes first (typically for emphasis) it is more usual to use the simple verb:

***Rather than** wake them, he let them sleep on.*

A few more examples will illustrate the point further:

*She encourages people to keep their jobs **rather than** [= instead of] dropping out to live in a commune.*
*Customers just 'pop in' **rather than** [= instead of] having to make a special journey.*

*He strode on ahead, **rather than** waiting for her to join him* [he did not wait for her].

There is a tendency to use the simple form of the verb that follows *rather than* when there is a sense of balance between the alternatives and the choice is more a matter of preference than of rejection:

*Perhaps you'd like to sit down **rather than** hover at the back.*
*Obviously one would like to make money **rather than** lose money.*
*I decided to stay overnight **rather than** wait for the last bus home.*
*Some Christians allowed themselves to be manipulated by the State, **rather than** face severe hardship or persecution.*

With passive forms of verbs, the participial *-ed* form of the verb is typically repeated:

*The allowance would be phased out gradually **rather than** ended abruptly.*

Repeating a link word, e.g. a preposition, can simplify matters by imposing an obligatory structure:

*The government should save money **by reducing** the benefits rather than **by abolishing** them.*
(The repetition of *by* makes another *-ing* form obligatory.)

reason is . . .

When *reason* is followed by a part of the verb *be* (typically *is* or *was*) and a clause, the linking word should be *that* and not *because*:

✗ *Even if he has made a mistake they are still bound by the price. The **reason is** because [✓ that] they have agreed to be bound by it.*

refer

See ALLUDE, REFER.

refute, repudiate

Take care not to use *refute* when you simply mean *repudiate*. To *refute* a proposition or allegation is to produce arguments that undermine it or destroy it, whereas to *repudiate* it is to reject or deny it (you can also use these words instead). In the first of the following examples *refute* is used appropriately, whereas in the second it is not:

✓ *I intend to spend as much time as I can **refuting** Carslake's idiotic principle.*
✗ *He now firmly **refutes** [✓ rejects, denies, repudiates] suggestions that he is unhappy with the Yorkshire set-up and is looking around for a move to another county.*

In no circumstances should *refute* be followed by a *that*-clause:

✗ *I **refute** that the County Council is unsympathetic to local concerns.*

regretful, regrettable

Regretful means 'feeling regret' and applies to a person, whereas *regrettable* means 'causing regret' and applies to an action or situation:

*We park the boat beside the tent, **regretful** at leaving the water.*

*I have apologized to your master for the **regrettable** error.*

Take care not to use the adverb *regretfully* (= in a regretful way, with regret) erroneously for *regrettably* (= as is to be regretted), especially as a sentence adverb:

✓ *Hands were shaken and drinks offered, **regretfully** [= with regret] refused by the policemen.*

✗ *You have to listen intelligently to the lecturer and think about what he is saying. **Regretfully** [✓ regrettably] not all students do this.*

repetitive, repetitious

Repetitive is much more common than *repetitious*, and the meanings differ slightly: *repetitive* is a more neutral word and means 'occurring repeatedly':

*The dancers in Greek theatre sang out the **repetitive** bits and encouraged the audience to join in.*

In less neutral contexts, *repetitive* tends to refer to the nature of the task or situation, whereas *repetitious* relates more to the performer of the task and implies an avoidable tedium:

*They are used to carrying out dull **repetitive** chores and filling out the endless paperwork that forms the major part of any intelligence operation.*

*In the same **repetitious** way she had recalled the scene she'd interrupted the evening before by announcing that supper was ready.*

replace, substitute

These words are complementary in describing the same process from different perspectives, and confusion can arise in choosing between *by* and *with* as the link word. The general pattern is:

A replaces B
You replace A **with** B
A is replaced **by** or **with** B
You substitute A **for** B
B is substituted **for** A

*The combination of computer and laser printer effectively **replaces** the work that would normally be carried out by a typesetter.*
*We miss meals and **replace** them **with** snacks which may mean missing out on vital nutrients.*
*The teds of the fifties **had been replaced by** the mods.*
*The driver's frown disappeared, **to be replaced with** a knowing, roguish grin.*
*The court should not **substitute** its own decision **for** that of the parent.*
*The technology that **has been substituted for** human lives on the widest scale is that of the microprocessor.*

Beware of using *substitute* when you mean *replace*:

✗ *It couldn't have been very nice for her to see her sister* **substituted** [✓ replaced] *by a woman who had obtained cheap success by such a blatant display of sexuality.*

✗ *If paper does not rot, why bother to* **substitute** *it* **for** [✓ replace it with] *plastic?*

replete

This word means 'filled or well supplied' with some necessity such as food. It is also used in abstract contexts and is typically followed by the preposition *with*:

The area of medical jurisprudence is **replete** *with such absurdities, which date from an earlier age when superstition was a substitute for knowledge.*

It should not be used as an alternative for *complete*, which shares this grammatical pattern:

✗ *A two-storey retirement home* **replete** [✓ complete] *with pool, bar and stuccoed façade.*

repudiate

See REFUTE, REPUDIATE.

respective, respectively

These are useful words in relating information to two or more items – whether named separately or collectively – and clarifying what applies to both and what applies to only one:

*The comparative advantages and disadvantages of the businesses are related to their **respective** growth characteristics.*

(Use of *respective* shows that each business had its own set of characteristics. Without it we might think that all the businesses displayed the same characteristics.)

*They tipped on to his desk their haul of three shotguns and a pistol for which the **respective** owners had no licences.*

(That is, each weapon had a distinct owner, instead of all the weapons being owned by one group of owners.)

*The children stayed in the creche until the age of six, when they were transferred to two other institutions for boys and girls **respectively**.*

(Use of *respectively* shows that one of the institutions was for boys and the other for girls. Without it we might think that both were mixed institutions.)

*The coffin furniture was usually quite plain, with simple grip-plates and grips typical of domestic furniture of the period, being of sheet iron and wrought iron **respectively**.*

(Grip-plates were made of sheet iron and grips were made of wrought iron.)

*The book has five parts, dealing **respectively** with the nature of intelligence and its measurement; cognition, personality, and intelligence; society, culture, and intelligence; the phylogeny and ontogeny of intelligence; and a metatheory of intelligence.*

(In this long list, which might well be presented in another form (e.g. as a table), *respectively* makes it clear at the outset that each chapter deals with one of the complex topics that follow.)

In some cases, however, the meaning is clear without them, and they are superfluous (*respective* in particular):

✗ *The company is catching up with IBM UK, he said, pointing to the **respective** performances of each.*
(*Each* is present to distinguish the two companies.)
✗ *She had outlived three husbands and gathered in their **respective** estates.*
✗ *This morning twenty-five thousand festival-goers began making their way back to their **respective** homes at the end of all points of the compass.*

In other cases, *respective(ly)* is logical and can improve the balance of the sentence, but the context makes the meaning obvious and it can be left out:

? *As time went on, Shanti and Chris began to visit each other's homes. When they were sixteen and eighteen **respectively**, they told us they wanted to be married.*
? *Delegations from the communist parties of Laos and Cambodia were led by their **respective** general secretaries.*

My boys, stand forward! Look here, sir; these children have been respectively named after our late sovereign, and the husband of our present queen.

William Thackeray, *Catherine*, 1839

revenge

See AVENGE, REVENGE.

scarcely

See BARELY, HARDLY, SCARCELY.

semicolon

See COLON *AND* SEMICOLON.

sensible, sensitive

The main meaning of *sensible* is 'having good sense', i.e. the opposite of 'foolish'; that of *sensitive* is 'easily offended or emotionally hurt'. They begin to overlap in meanings involving emotional or sensual reaction: you are *sensible of* something when you are aware of it emotionally (typically as involving someone else: *we're all very sensible of the strain of your situation*) and are *sensitive to* it when it affects you in the physical senses or emotionally (*sensitive to cold, always shivering / sensitive to criticism*). But *sensible of* now sounds dated, and *conscious of* or *aware of* would be the more natural choice, especially when the perception is more intellectual than emotional.

There is greater difficulty with the nouns *sensibility* and *sensitivity*. *Sensibility* corresponds to *sensible* (in its familiar meaning) much less closely than *sensitivity* does to *sensitive*, and is related chiefly to an individual's finer feelings (often in the plural):

*Tell your friend I'm sorry I offended her **sensibilities.***

Sensitivity has a wider range of meanings concerned with physical or emotional reactions of various kinds, or with the capacity for these:

*He still moved her with his intelligence, his charm, his **sensitivity**.*
*It is quite right that members' **sensitivities** should be aired.*

sensual, sensuous

The older word is *sensual*, which essentially describes feelings involving the senses as distinct from the intellect. Over time it has become more closely associated with sexual and other forms of physical desire (such as indulgence in food), and *sensuous*, which Milton appears to have coined in the 1640s, took over the meanings that specifically related to aesthetic rather than carnal feelings. This distinction is still useful:

*The kiss was light, sensitive, and softly **sensual**.*
*She flushed, almost as if he could have known the part he'd played in her extraordinarily **sensual** dreams.*
*The language here is very **sensuous** and more physical than the last stanzas.*

Words that are so similar in form and close in their range of meaning will always get in each other's way (typically *sensuous* used for *sensual*), and it is not difficult to find examples that violate this rule. But it is useful to bear it in mind when using these words yourself.

sexism

See GENDER *AND* GENDER-NEUTRALITY.

shall *and* will, should *and* would

The main uses of *shall* and *will* are to express something that will exist or happen in the future (*shall/will explain it all shortly*) and to express a purpose or instruction (*shall/will not tolerate such behaviour*). In everyday speech, *shall* and *will* are normally contracted into the pronoun that comes before it (*I'll, you'll, she'll, they'll,* etc.) and then the distinction between the two forms becomes irrelevant. When you have to use the words in full, you have to make a choice:

- in more formal writing, when the contracted forms might appear too casual.
- in questions and negatives (*shall I?, will you?,* etc. / *shall not, will not, shan't, won't*).

The traditional distinction in use between *shall* and *will* in British English (outside Scotland), is that *shall* is used in the first person (with *I* and *we*) to make simple statements relating to future time, and in questions to express a tentative suggestion or invitation, and *will* is used in the second and third persons:

*I **shall** have more to say about this in due course.*
***Shall** we talk about it over a drink?*
*If you comply you **will** be rewarded.*
*VAT **will** not be imposed on books or newspapers.*
*What **will** they want to do about it?*

To express an intention or instruction, the opposite applies: *will* is used in the first person, and *shall* in the second and third persons:

*I **will** never go there again.*
*'I'll do it.' 'So you **shall**.'*
*Visitors **shall** report to the duty officer.*

In practice, however, the meaning distinction between simple future statements and statements of intention is often hazy, and *will* tends to be used in almost all cases, *shall* being largely confined to first-person use when there is a strong element of intention.

Shall is less versatile, and is not idiomatic in the second and third persons in statements and questions that deal with simple information rather than expressing intention or instruction (✘ *What **shall** they want to do about it?*).

USAGE NOTE – In Scottish English, and also in the English of Ireland and America, it is normal practice to use *will* in all cases, even in the first person when in British English *shall* is used:

Will *I show you to your room?*

Should *and* would

These forms are used mainly to form past tenses (*I knew it would be unpleasant*), express a wish or request (*I should like to go / would you join me?*), and in conditional *if*-clauses (*they wouldn't object if we asked them*).

Traditionally, *should* and *would* have the same distinction in use that *shall* and *will* have when referring to future action, *should* being used with *I* and *we*, and *would* being used with the second and third persons. In practice, however, *would* is often used in all these cases.

This usage is complicated by the fact that *should* has special roles not shared by *would* but corresponding to meanings of *ought to* and *must*, expressing obligation or probability (*You should do what we say / the meal should be ready soon*). To avoid confusion with these meanings, it is usually better to use *would* and not *should* in the first person:

*I **would** have told them if they had seemed at all interested.*

For a fuller treatment of these words, see *How to Write Better English*, pp. 24–8.

situation

This is a useful word to convey the meaning 'a set of circumstances, a state of affairs', especially with a defining adjective, e.g. *the economic situation*, *the present situation*, etc. It is more controversial when a noun precedes: *emergency situation* means no more than plain *emergency*, which denotes a situation in itself. When the preceding noun is not a 'situation' word, however, it can still be useful: *hostage situation* is a convenient way of saying 'a situation in which hostages have been taken'.

slither, sliver

Slither is a verb meaning 'to slip or slide unsteadily', whereas *sliver* is a noun meaning 'a thin narrow piece cut off a larger piece'. They are often confused (usually *slither* for *sliver*).

sociable, social

These two words relate to different meanings of *society*. *Social* is a classifying word that is concerned with the relation of human beings to one another (*a social being* / *a social occasion*). A *social worker* caters for people in society who need help, and *social security* is financial help given to such people.

Sociable is an evaluative word corresponding to *society* in the sense 'companionship, good company' and relates to the quality of human relations. A *sociable* person is friendly and socially active and competent, and a *sociable* occasion is one that people enjoy.

sort of

See KIND OF, SORT OF.

specially

See ESPECIALLY, SPECIALLY.

specious, spurious

Specious originally meant 'having a fine appearance' (from Latin *species* 'outward form'), but in the seventeenth century it developed the unfavourable sense 'superficially persuasive but wrong' as in *a specious argument. Spurious*, which is sometimes confused with *specious*, is derived from the Latin adjective *spurius* 'false', and means 'not genuine, not being what it purports to be'. It used to mean 'illegitimate' with reference to a child, but this meaning is obsolete. In current usage, a *specious* claim is an outwardly attractive but insubstantial one whereas a *spurious* claim is based on a false premiss.

speed

When *speed* means 'to move or travel fast', the past tense and past participle are *sped* (*The train sped towards the tunnel / They had sped upstairs*). When the meaning is 'to break a speed limit' or when the verb is transitive (taking an object), the form is *speeded* (*had speeded to get there in time / a process that needs to be speeded up*). *Sped* is often preferred in AmE in this second group.

spelling problems

Some quite short words cause as much trouble as the long complicated ones. Here is a list of the most common short words that tend to be spelt wrongly:

beige	height	seize
chief	juice	siege
eighth	niece	strength
gauge	pierce	twelfth
guard	priest	weird

Most spelling difficulties, however, occur in long words. Here is a list of the words that cause most trouble:

abbreviation	affiliate	answer
abhorrence	affiliated	apologize
abscess	affiliation	apostasy
accelerator	aggravate	appalling
accessible	aggression	apparently
accessory	aggressive	arbitrary
accommodate	aghast	archaeology
accommodation	alignment	artefact
accompaniment	allegation	asphalt
achievement	allege	asphyxiate
acknowledgement	allegedly	assassin
acquaint	allotment	assassinate
acquaintance	almond	asthma
acquiesce	ambidextrous	attach
acquire	amphitheatre	attachment
acquit	anaesthetic	attendant
address	analyse	autumn
adequate	anemone	ayatollah (Iranian
advantageous	annihilate	religious leader)
advertise	annihilation	bachelor
advertisement	annul	bankruptcy
aerial	annulment	barbecue
aerosol	anonymous	bazaar

beautiful

beginner

beginning

behaviour

belief

believe

beneficent

berserk

biased

billionaire

biscuit

bourgeois

breathalyse

broccoli

budgeting

buoyant

bureaucracy

burglar

caffeine

calendar (of dates)

camouflage

cannabis

caress

carriage

cassette

catalogue

catarrh

cauliflower

cemetery

chameleon

champagne

changeable

cigarette

clientele

coconut

coercion

collaborate

collapsible

colossal

commemorate

commiserate

commitment

committed

committee

comparative

compatible

compel

compelling

competent

conceive

conference

connection

connoisseur

conscientious

consensus

controversy

convalesce

convalescence

cooperate

cooperation

cooperative

copier

counterfeit

courageous

cupful

curriculum

cylinder

deceive

definite

dependant (noun)

dependent
   (adjective)

descendant

desiccated

desperate

detach

detachment

diaphragm

diarrhoea

diphtheria

diphthong

disappear

disappearance

disappoint

disappointed

disappointment

disapprove

dispatch (*despatch*
   is also correct)

dispel

dissect

dissipate

ecstasy

effervesce

efficient

eligible

embarrass
embarrassed
embarrassment
encyclopedia
   (*encyclopaedia* is
   also correct)
endeavour
enrol
enrolment
enthral
equipment
equipped
euthanasia
exaggerate
exasperate
exceed
excellent
excerpt
exercise
exhibition
exhilarate
extraordinary
extravagant
extrovert
fascinate
February
fetus (*foetus* is
   also correct)
fledgling
   (*fledgeling* is
   also correct)
fluorescent

foreign
foreigner
forfeit
fulfil
generation
ghastly
ghetto
giraffe
government
graffiti
grandad
granddaughter
grievous
guarantee
guaranteed
guardian
guillotine
gymnastics
gypsy
haemorrhage
hallucination
handful
handicap
handkerchief
harass
harassed
harassment
hereditary
honorary
honourable
humorous
hygiene

hygienic
hypochondriac
hypocrisy
idiosyncrasy
illegitimate
illiterate
impostor
inadvertent
inconceivable
independent
   (adjective and
   noun)
indispensable
infallible
innocuous
inseparable
install
instalment
interrogate
interrogation
interrupt
interruption
invisible
irascible
irreplaceable
irresistible
irresponsible
irritable
jeopardize
jewellery
   (*jewelry* is also
   correct)

judgement
   (*judgment* is
   also correct)
keenness
khaki
kidnapper
kilometre
lackadaisical
lacquer
languor
latish (= fairly late)
lecherous
leisure
leopard
liaise
liaison
library
lieutenant
liquefy
literature
luscious
macabre
macaroon
magnanimous
maintenance
manageable
manoeuvre
marijuana
marmalade
marriage
martyr
marvellous

massacre
mayonnaise
medicine
medieval
mellifluous
memento
mileage (*milage* is
   also correct)
millennium
millionaire
miniature
minuscule
miscellaneous
mischievous
misshapen
misspell
moccasin
mortgage
moustache
mouthful
Muhammad
naive (*naïve* is also
   correct)
necessary
negligent
negligible
noticeable
nuisance
obscene
occasionally
occurrence
omelette

omission
omit
omitted
opponent
paediatric
paedophile
paraffin
parallel
paralleled
parliament
perceive
permanent
perseverance
persevere
pharaoh
pigeon
plausible
Portuguese
precede
preceding
preferable
prejudice
prerogative
proceed
pronunciation
pseudonym
psychology
pygmy
pyjamas
pyramid
quarrelsome
questionnaire

queuing
rarefy
receipt
receive
recommend
reconnaissance
redundant
refrigerator
regrettable
relieve
reminiscence
remittance
reservoir
responsible
restaurant
restaurateur
resuscitate
rheumatism
rhythm
Romanian
sacrilege
sacrilegious
sandwich
sausage
scavenge
schizophrenia
secretary
separate
sergeant (military)
Shakespeare
shepherd

signature
silhouette
simultaneous
skilful
solemn
somersault
sovereign
spaghetti
spoonful
steadfast
subtle
subtlety
subtly
successful
suddenness
superintendent
supersede
supplement
suppress
surveillance
susceptible
sustenance
synagogue
syringe
targeted
tariff
tattoo
temperament
temperamental
temperature
temporarily

temporary
terrible
thinness
threshold
tranquillity
transferable
traveller
treacherous
typical
unconscious
uncooperative
unforgettable
unforgivable
unnecessary
unwieldy
vacuum
vegetable
vehicle
vengeance
verruca
veterinary
Wednesday
whether
wholly
withhold
woollen
woolly
worshipper
yoghurt (*yogurt* is
    also correct)
zoology

split infinitives

The infinitive of a verb is the simple form that is used, for example, as the headword in a dictionary: *break, come, do,* etc. as distinct from the inflected forms *breaks, broke, broken, came, done,* and so on. Some verbs, especially those that express a wish or obligation, are used with the infinitive of other verbs and need the word *to* before it: *I want* **to see,** *We like* **to walk,** *There is no need* **to shout,** *It is wrong* **to kill people.** This type is known as a *to*-infinitive.

A split infinitive occurs when you need a *to*-infinitive and a word or phrase comes between *to* and the verb:

I know too that **to repeatedly drink and drive** *is a profound and serious matter.*

The only way you can make an impression on such a person is **to calmly pour** *a glass of water all over his meat and two veg in the works canteen.*

HISTORICAL NOTE – Infinitives have been split since Middle English (the form of English in use from the twelfth century, after the Norman Conquest) and in the nineteenth century it came back into favour. Nobody objected to splitting a *to*-infinitive until relatively recently, and the term itself is not found until the end of the nineteenth century. There is a famous example in Byron:

To sit on rocks to muse o'er flood and fell, **To slowly trace** *the forest's shady scene.*

Childe Harold's Pilgrimage, 1812

There is no good basis in grammar for insisting on keeping the two parts of an infinitive together. The argument that *to* and the verb form a unit does not accord with other verb patterns in English, in which parts of a verb are separated (for example, *I have never agreed* and *They are always complaining*). Avoidance of a split infinitive is rather a matter of style, and other typical patterns of word order come into play.

The normal position for an adverb is often before or after the *to*-infinitive, not within it:

? *I used to **always** climb in with my girlfriend on a Saturday night.*

The normal order is:

✓ *I used **always** to climb in with my girlfriend on a Saturday night.*

The adverb can come after the infinitive when the sense allows this:

✓ *Everyone expected things **to improve immediately**.*

However, there are cases where the adverb or adverb phrase belongs closely to the verb, typically when it has a moderating or intensifying role:

✓ *The government is seeking **to gradually reduce** the burden of direct taxation on this income group.*
✓ *The Education Secretary has set out proposals **to radically change** the way in which pupils apply for university places.*
✓ *A nineteenth-century restorer attempted to remove the paint in order **to fully reveal** the trees in the background.*
✓ *The cost is likely **to more than double**.*

(In the first three sentences, the adverbs could be put after the infinitives, i.e. *to reduce gradually*, *to change radically*, and *to reveal fully*, but the emphasis is changed and the flow of the sentence is poorer. In the last sentence, *more than double* is in effect a compound verb.)

There are two particular circumstances in which it is best to avoid a split infinitive, because the split is clumsy or awkward:

• when the part that comes between is a phrase:

✗ *You two shared a curious ability **to without actually saying anything make** me feel dirty.*

• when a negative or limiting word such as *not*, *never*, *scarcely*, goes with the infinitive:

✗ *We hoped **to never need** them again.*
✓ *We hoped **never to need** them again.*
✓ *We **never hoped** to need them again.*

stationary, stationery

Both words are derived from the Latin word *stare* 'to stand'. *Stationary* is an adjective and means 'having a fixed position, not moving'; *stationery* is a noun and means 'materials used for writing'. The medieval Latin word *stationarius* meant 'a bookseller', who was a fixed (as distinct from itinerant) shopkeeper.

stop

See CEASE, STOP.

subjunctives

The subjunctive is a special form (or mood) of a verb expressing a wish or possibility instead of fact. It is still used in English (especially American English), but its role has tended to become limited to contexts in which the element of possibility needs to be emphasized:

*Duval was allowed to visit Réunion, on condition that he **return** by April 30.*

*When he first arrived, people called him Johnny, but he's since insisted that he **be addressed** as John.*

In these sentences, the verbs *return* (in the first) and *be addressed* (in the second) are in the subjunctive; the ordinary forms (called the indicative) would be *returns* and *is addressed*. The subjunctive form is recognizable in English only in the third person singular present tense, which omits the final -s, and in the forms *be* and *were* of the verb *be*.

In many cases, an alternative construction with *should* or *might* can also be used, and in some cases a simple form of the verb (e.g. *is* instead of *be*):

*He's since insisted that he **should be addressed** as John.*

Other typical uses of the subjunctive are given below. In most cases alternative non-subjunctive structures have become standard:

• after *if* (or *as if*, *as though*, or *unless*) in open conditions:

*He would be welcome back in Pakistan if he **were chosen** for England's next tour there.*
(Also possible: *if he was chosen . . .*)

• in negative constructions, with *not* (or *never* etc.) normally placed before the subjunctive verb, so that the subjunctive status of the verb is recognizable in the first and second persons as well as the third:

*He suggested that we not **make** any further comment.*
(Also possible: *. . . that we should not make any further comment.*)
*One essential quality for a holiday novel is that it not **be** too light.*
(Also possible: *. . . that it should not be too light.*)

• in certain fixed expressions and phrases, e.g. *as it were, be that as it may, come what may, far be it from me, God save the Queen, heaven forbid, perish the thought, so be it.*
• in 'unreal' conditions, i.e. those that are not or could not be the case:

*What would he do **if he were** (or **was**) in my place?*
***If I were you** I would get a little dog.*

The last example illustrates the common idiom *if I were you. Were* is a survival of the English subjunctive, and is also used in the first example, although there you could use *was* instead.

• *be* or *were* placed at the beginning of a clause with

the subject following it, expressing a condition equivalent to an *if*-clause:

Rulers who let their hearts rule their heads tend to court disaster, **be** *they male or female.*
(Also possible: *whether they are male or female.*)
One gentleman said to her that, **were** *she* **to run** *such a boarding house in England and charge what she charged in Florence, she would be besieged.*
(Also possible: *If she was to run . . .*)

such as

See LIKE, SUCH AS.

substitute

See REPLACE, SUBSTITUTE.

superstitions

A language superstition, like any superstition, is a firmly held belief that has no reasonable or logical basis. Many of them arose in the eighteenth and nineteenth centuries, when self-appointed guardians of the language started to write new rules which were largely based on their knowledge of Latin grammar and had little to do with the ways of English: that you should not end a sentence with a preposition (e.g. *the chair is for sitting on*), that *different* should be followed by *from* because you say *differ from* (even though we say *accord with* but *according to*); that *none* should always be followed by a singular verb; that a sentence should not begin with *and* or *but*, and others. (Many sentences in this book begin that way, and the author makes no apology for them.) The best-known superstition of all is the one that condemns the split infinitive, discussed a little further back in this book.

Earlier generations also had their superstitions, most of which have long since vanished into the mists of usage. In the eighteenth century, Dr Johnson listed among his dislikes what he called 'low words'; these included *bogus, coax, joke, flog, prim, rogue, snob,* and *spree*, all of which are now accepted items of general vocabulary. Henry Fowler, the author of *A Dictionary of Modern English Usage*, published in 1926, had his list too, among them *cachet, caption, coastal,* and *malnutrition*, all of them once again familiar words now. He also insisted that words formed on Latin plurals, such as *agenda* and *data*, should be used as plural nouns. Since then, *agenda* has developed a meaning that makes it a singular noun (e.g. *The agenda has been circulated*), and *data*, a word transformed by the computer age, is going the same way.

systematic, systemic

Systematic is the more common and versatile of these two words, basically meaning 'done according to a plan or system' (*systematic learning, a systematic search*, etc.). The less common word *systemic* means 'common to a system or organization as a whole (rather than part of it)', as in *systemic failures*. *Systemic* also has special technical uses in medicine and linguistics.

tautology

This term is derived from Greek words meaning 'same' and 'word'. It denotes a form of word redundancy in which the same idea or meaning is expressed more than once in a phrase or sentence, as in *a new innovation*, and *to return back*. Some tautologies have become idiomatic (e.g. *free gift* and *past history*) and it is pointless to object to them.

Tautologies that involve words that can be removed from writing without altering or weakening the meaning should be avoided (these words are shown in bold type):

✗ *Two of their peers were electrocuted **to death** while fleeing police.*

✗ *The conference reached its **final** climax this morning.*

✗ *Security guards kept **unwanted** gatecrashers from scaling the high wire fence.*

their, there, they're

Their is the third-person plural possessive pronoun (*their opinion is of no interest*). *There* is an adverb meaning 'to or in that place' (*put it there / we live there*) and is also used idiomatically with *is* and *are* (*there is no more to be said / there were three of them*). *They're* is a contraction of 'they are' (*they're no use any more*). The most common mistake, aggravated partly by the practice in text-messaging, is to use *there* for *they're*.

theirs

There is no apostrophe: *this work of theirs.*

themselves, themself

The standard reflexive form of *they* and *them* is *themselves* (*Some people have made fools of themselves*), and this is widely used as a gender-neutral form in the same way as *they* and *their* are (*anyone who involves themselves in such issues*). An old form *themself* has recently come back into use as a gender-neutral word (*a person who cannot make decisions for themself*), but until it becomes more widely accepted it should only be used informally.

they, them, their

These third-person plural pronouns have been used for several centuries to refer back to a singular indefinite word such as *anyone, everyone, nobody, someone,* etc.:

*If someone comes in, **they** will have to wait.*
*Every tutor has a right to **their** own methods.*
*Before you employ a babysitter, ask **them** into your home and find out about them.*

This usage is established and legitimate, and its value has been increased in recent years by the need to find a gender-neutral option in place of more awkward conventions such as *he or she, his or her,* and so on.

though

See ALTHOUGH, THOUGH.

tight, tightly

Like *flat* (see above), *tight* has two adverb forms: *tight* and *tightly*. *Tight* is used with a number of verbs (*hold tight, sit tight, sleep tight*), and as part of certain compound adjectives (*tight-fisted, tight-fitting, tight-knit, tight-lipped, tight shut*).

In general use, *tightly* is the correct form:

*She lay rigid for a count of ten, eyes **tightly** closed.*
*All glues need to be **tightly** clamped while they set.*
*His arms held her **tightly** to him, as if never wanting to let her go.*

till

See UNTIL, TILL.

titillate, titivate

Titillate is derived from Latin *titillare* 'to tickle' and means 'to excite' and often has sexual overtones, especially in the derived noun *titillation*:

*It's all polished and pacy enough to **titillate** a teen audience.*
*The reports are typically sensational and **titillating**.*
*The clear purpose of the extensive news coverage was **titillation**.*

Titivate, which probably originates as a blend of *tidy* and *cultivate* or *renovate*, means 'to adorn or smarten':

*She hoped he wasn't **titivating** himself, slicking his hair and freshening his breath.*

When there is a confusion, it is usually *titivate* mistakenly used for *titillate*.

tortuous, torturous

Both words are derived from Latin *torquere* meaning 'to twist', but their literal meanings are different. *Tortuous* means 'twisting and winding' (*a tortuous route / a tortuous process*), whereas *torturous* relates directly to the noun *torture* and means 'extremely painful' (*were running at a torturous pace*). They both have figurative uses in the sense 'extremely difficult or complex', and it is here that the overlap is most obvious. *Tortuous* language is convoluted and poorly structured, whereas *torturous* language is painful (literally, 'torture') to read; these may be two aspects of the same thing but the meanings are different. On the whole, when there is such a choice, *tortuous* is the more familiar and preferable word.

transpire

Transpire is derived from a Latin word meaning 'to breathe', and its proper meaning is 'to leak out, to become known'. It should not be used as an alternative for *occur* or *happen*:

✓ It **transpires** that Ram got on a plane in Kansas City, looked out of the window and got straight back off again.

✓ Violet, it **transpired**, had returned from the city because her father was dying.

✗ Everything that has **transpired** [✓ happened or occurred] in this room has been recorded.

✗ If it **transpires** [✓ happens] that the patient has not yet attended the general practitioner for this diabetic review one reminder prompt is sent.

(The meaning here is not 'becomes known' but 'happens', and 'if it happens that' is equivalent to 'in the event that', i.e. it relates to the fact itself and not to knowledge of it.)

trillion

See BILLON, TRILLION.

troop, troupe

A *troop* is a unit of armoured soldiers or of Scouts, or in extended use any group of similar people or animals, whereas a *troupe* is a company of actors or performers. Similarly, a *trooper* is a soldier (and, in America and Australia, a mounted police officer) and a *trouper* is a member of a group of actors or performers or (figuratively) 'a loyal and dependable person' (*Maisie proved to be a real trouper – just like her mum*).

underestimate

See OVERESTIMATE, UNDERESTIMATE.

uninterested

See DISINTERESTED, UNINTERESTED.

unique

? *The traditional Indian kitchen is **fairly unique**. For example, in India, saucepans do not have handles.*

A sentence like this can annoy language purists: surely, they argue, if *unique* means 'not like any other person or thing', its meaning is absolute and invariable, and nothing can be *fairly* unique. Nor, for that matter, can it be *rather unique* or *somewhat unique*, let alone *very unique* or *extremely unique*. But the argument is philosophical rather than linguistic: it is based on logic and not grammar. Indeed, even in these terms it is misconceived. In the sentence above, the implication is that the Indian kitchen is unique in some ways but not others: it has saucepans, for example, but the saucepans have no handles. The kitchen might be even more unique if it didn't have saucepans at all, and it would only be totally unique if it differed in every respect from its European counterpart (which is hard to imagine).

Language is governed by idiom and not logic: linguistically, it is still idiomatic to qualify *unique*, as with *perfect* and other theoretically absolute concepts:

*It is a chance for people to see a **rather unique** private collection of art.*

*The game pits your modern soldiers against hordes of orcs, wizards and undead – a **fairly unique** idea in itself.*

> *This butterfly, this plaything, this bridal-gift of a poor watchmaker to a blacksmith's wife, was, in truth, a gem of art that a monarch would have purchased with honors and abundant wealth, and have treasured it among the jewels of his kingdom, as the most unique and wondrous of them all!*
>
> Nathaniel Hawthorne, *Mosses from an Old Manse*, 1846

unsatisfied

See DISSATISFIED, UNSATISFIED.

unsociable, unsocial

Like the positive forms (see SOCIABLE, SOCIAL), *unsocial* is a classifying word. It essentially means 'not suitable for or compatible with society', and is commonly used in the context of work (*unsocial hours*). It can be used of a person in the sense 'disliking social activity or company', but the more usual word in this range of meaning is *unsociable*. Another word, *antisocial*, means 'contrary to or harmful to the social order' (with reference to people and activities, as in *antisocial behaviour*) and has more sinister implications.

until, till

Till is the older word and not a shortening of *until*, in which the *un-* element is an intensifying prefix meaning 'up to' or 'as far as'. The two words are largely interchangeable, but there are a few special points to note:

• *Until* is more usual at the beginning of a sentence:

__Until__ it is shown that the tape is genuine, we have to remain sceptical.

• *Till* is most effective when followed by a simple noun:

They danced almost __till__ dawn.

• *Till* has a more informal tone, especially when used as a conjunction (followed by a clause with a verb) and *until* is often preferred for this reason:

The sun came out and dried the heather __till__ it crackled.
The clerk waited __till__ Ranulf returned.

She walked on __until__ she reached Starr Hills.
Her parents had done birthday parties on a grand scale __until__ she was about thirteen.

urban, urbane

It is easy to confuse these two words, which are derived from the same Latin root *urbs, urbis* meaning 'city'. *Urban* means 'relating to cities and towns' and is typically used in contrast with *rural* (*the urban landscape / urban deprivation*). *Urbane* is used of people in the sense 'suave and sophisticated' (originally, like a city-dweller) and is generally complimentary in tone.

valueless

See INVALUABLE.

venal, venial

These two words are unrelated in origin but close enough in form to cause confusion. *Venal* (from Latin *venum* 'thing for sale') means 'open to corrupt influence, bribable' and is used of people and their actions (*a venal political establishment*). *Venial* (from Latin *venia* 'pardon') means 'able to be pardoned, forgivable' and is used of sins and trangressions that are minor as distinct from mortal sins which bring eternal damnation.

verbal

See ORAL, VERBAL.

very, much

Very and *much* have complementary functions as intensifying adverbs:

• *Very* qualifies adjectives and adverbs: *very pleasant*, *very wide*, *very unfortunately*.
• *Much* qualifies the past participles of verbs used as

adjectives, especially when they come before a noun: *a much enlarged edition, a much complained-of decision*.

But the roles can overlap, because there is a considerable grey area in which some past participles, such as *alarmed, complicated, restricted, strained*, and *worried*, have become remote from their verb origins and have taken on the role of adjectives in their own right. In these cases *very* is the usual qualifier to use: *very alarmed* and *very worried* are idiomatic forms whereas *much alarmed* sounds dated and *much worried* is impossibly stilted and unidiomatic.

In some cases there is a choice because the verbal and adjectival roles are more finely balanced. For example, *a much honoured politician* implies a continuing process, whereas *a very honoured politician* suggests the current state of affairs.

The following examples, using *much* as the intensifier, all imply processes, with the verb aspect predominant:

*The social power of the squirearchy had been **much reduced**.*
*'Family life', by which is meant the life of the nuclear family, is **much praised** in government statements.*
*For some, the Kaiser was a most charming man, **much** misunderstood.*

In the following examples, use of *very* implies states, with the adjective aspect predominant:

*The software situation today is **very muddled**.*
*He felt **very involved** in the affair.*
*She seemed too tired to be **very interested**.*

waive, wave

Be sure to use the form *waive* for the verb meaning 'to refrain from demanding or enforcing (a right, claim, etc.)', and not *wave*, which is the more common word in meanings to do with sweeping the arms, flourishing things, greetings, and so on, and (as a noun) a ridge or swell in water, hair, etc.

weave

There are two words with this spelling, with meanings that overlap when used figuratively: (1) to do with forming cloth on a loom, from Old English, and (2) meaning 'to take a winding course', a later word from Old Norse. Because the two verbs have different sets of inflection — (1) has a past form *wove* and a past participle *woven*, and (2) has *weaved* for both — care needs to be taken to distinguish them in figurative uses. Both words can be used but the image is different in each case:

He **wove** his Ferrari in and out of traffic with an abandon that kept Caroline pinned back in her seat.
He punched the air and yelled something as he **weaved** from side to side across the road, zig-zagging into the distance
Climbers had **woven** their way into the timber railings.

The image in the first and third examples is of cloth-making; in the second example it is of following a winding course.

were, was

See SUBJUNCTIVES.

whatever, what ever

Whatever is written as one word when it is an indefinite relative pronoun or adjective used in statements or commands:

Whatever you're doing, a short break will help you to do it better.

We need to take a stand against racism in whatever form it arises.

It is also used as one word in the sense 'regardless of what':

Whatever else you might say about him, he believed in things and he did what he thought was proper.

It is also used informally with the continuation omitted:

There are bays next to the disk drive lying vacant waiting for CD-ROM drives, bigger hard disks or whatever.

Whatever is also the correct form when used as an adverb to strengthen negative statements:

I have no need whatever to rush into anything.

What ever is written as two words when *ever* retains its separate identity as an intensifying word, typically in questions:

What ever *put such an idea into your head?*

As a guide, if you can substitute *what on earth* or *what in heaven's name* or a similar variant for *what ever*, you need to spell *what ever* as two words.

who *and* whom

> *A certain young man never knew*
> *Just when to say* whom *and when* who;
> *'The question of choosing,'*
> *He said, 'is confusing;*
> *I wonder if* which *wouldn't do?'*
>
> Christopher Morley, *Mince Pie*, 1919

Who is used as a relative pronoun (*the person who paid us*) and as an interrogative (in questions: *who told you that?*). *Whom* is the objective form of *who*, used as the object of verbs and prepositions (*the person whom I met / the woman to whom I spoke / Whom did they want?*).

In practice, *whom* is disappearing, especially in everyday English:

• In questions it is giving way to *who*: *Who did they want?*

• In relative clauses it is either replaced by *that* or omitted altogether: *the person that I met* or *the person I met*.

• With prepositions, it is normal to omit *who* (or *that*) and place the preposition at the end: *the person I spoke to*. Using a preposition before *whom* can sound stilted and over-formal:

? *I am not sure for* **whom** *this package has been left.*

A mixed style with *whom* and a preposition at the end is also unsatisfactory:

✗ *I am not sure* **whom** *this package has been left for.*
✓ *I am not sure* **who** *this package has been left for.*

A common mistake is to prefer *whom* when *who* is in fact correct. This occurs in more complex relative clauses in which *who* seems to have a dual role:

✗ *You have to ask how many people are in mental institutions* **whom** *professionals think are harmless.*
✓ *You have to ask how many people are in mental institutions* **who** *professionals think are harmless.*

In this sentence, *whom* is not the object of the verb *think* but the subject of the clause *are harmless.* The words *professionals think* form a kind of aside, as is clear if we separate it with punctuation:

✓ *You have to ask how many people are in mental institutions who – professionals think – are harmless.*

Note also constructions in which a whole clause introduced by *who* is the object of a verb or preposition (in this case, *about*):

✗ *There was a long discussion about* **whom** *should lead the project.*
✓ *There was a long discussion about* **who** *should lead the project.*

The preposition *about* appears to be governing the relative pronoun *who(m)*, and so we might expect *whom* to be correct, but in fact *about* is governing the whole clause *who should lead the project*, and within this clause the pronoun *who* is the subject of the verb *should lead*, and not (by itself) the object of *about*.

whoever, who ever, whomever

The same distinction applies to *whoever* and *who ever* as to *whatever* and *what ever*. *Whoever* is written as one word when it is equivalent to 'whatever person' used in statements or commands (*Whoever wants it can have it*) and when the meaning is 'regardless of whom' (*Whoever it is, I don't want to see them*).

Who ever is written as two words when the expression as a whole is equivalent to *who on earth*, *who in heaven's name*, and so on, typically in questions: *Who ever are those people?*

The objective form *whomever* can sound formal or affected:

*Individuals are free to contract or not to contract with **whomever** they please.*

More often than not it is used wrongly:

✗ *I favour the downward position for the fork, protecting **whomever** picks up the plate from being spiked.*

(The verb *protecting* governs the whole clause including *picks up the plate*, and the pronoun is the subject of this clause: therefore it should be *whoever*.)

who's *and* whose

Who's is a contracted form of *who is* or *who has*, used in conversational and less formal written English. It is used for both roles of *who*, as a relative pronoun and as an interrogative pronoun (in questions):

(relative) *It's not been decided **who's** [= who is] going to be there.*
(relative) *We wonder **who's** [= who has] been doing these things.*
(interrogative) ***Who's** [= who is] that over there?*
(interrogative) ***Who's** [= who has] done this?*

Take care to avoid confusing this use with the pronoun and determiner *whose*, which is used to show possession and is also both relative and interrogative:

(relative) *There were people **whose** families had died in the bombing.*
(interrogative) ***Whose** car is parked outside?*

won't, wont

Won't, with an apostrophe, is a contraction of *will not* used informally (*I won't do it / Won't you come with us?*). *Wont* (with no apostrophe) is a literary word used as a noun and adjective to denote custom or habit (*places where people are wont to meet / as was their wont*).

your, you're

Beware of confusing the possessive word *your* (*is this your bag?*) with the contraction *you're* meaning 'you are' (*surely you're not serious*). Using *your* to mean 'you are' is common in text-messaging, where abbreviation serves a useful purpose, but in other forms of language use it is illiterate.

yours

There is no apostrophe: *this work of yours.*

zeugma

Avoid constructions in which a word, or a particular form of a word, belongs grammatically to two parts of the sentence but is strictly correct only in one:

✗ *I believe we have and should continue to make every effort.* (*to make* fits with *should continue* but not with *have*, which calls for *made*)
✓ *I believe we have made and should continue to make every effort.*

Structures such as this are technically ungrammatical, and should be confined to everyday conversation where the pragmatics of language makes them occasionally inevitable. They sometimes occur in literature for special effect and are known as *zeugma* (pronounced **zyoog**-ma, from a Greek word for 'yoking').

This type of structure is discussed more fully in *How to Write Better English*, p. 174.

Glossary

This glossary includes the terms most often used in the course of this book. Cross-references are to other items in the glossary.

absolute an absolute adjective is one used without a following noun, e.g. *the poor*.

abstract noun a noun that names an abstract quality, state, or activity, e.g. *anger, hunting, loneliness, statement, warmth*. See also **concrete noun**.

active the form of a verb in which the subject performs the action and the object (if any) is affected by the action, e.g. *She parked the car; A man stood in the doorway*. See also **passive**.

adjective a word that describes a person or thing, e.g. *a red hat, an Italian meal, the room is square*.

adverb a word that tells you how or where or when an action is done, e.g. *She smiled gently; He went downstairs; Tomorrow we'll go swimming*.

adverbial *or* adverb phrase a phrase that has the role of an adverb, e.g. *down the road, in the morning, in any way you can*.

affirmative an affirmative verb or sentence states a fact that is the case, or is equivalent to the answer 'yes'. See also **negative**.

agreement   use of the correct forms of words when they relate to each other in a sentence, e.g. changing *have* to *has* in the sentence *He has a lot to answer for.*

ambiguity   using words in a way that can produce more than one possible meaning, e.g. *Will you check their progress?*

antecedent   the word or phrase in a sentence to which a later word, especially a pronoun, refers, e.g. **The person** *waved his hand* (*the person* is the antecedent of *his*).

attributive   an attributive adjective or noun is one that is placed before another word, typically a noun, so as to qualify it in some way, e.g. *a **bright** moon, an **expiry** date.* See also **predicative.**

auxiliary verbs   the verbs *be, do,* and *have,* and the modal verbs *can, could, may, might, must, shall, should, will,* and *would,* all of which are used to make forms of other verbs, e.g. *be going, do like, have seen, can sleep,* etc.

clause   a group of words containing a verb and its subject. A main clause makes sense by itself and can form a complete sentence, e.g. *I'll write them a letter.* A subordinate clause does not make complete sense by itself and is attached to a main clause, e.g. *I'll write them a letter **if I have the time**.*

collective noun   a noun that refers to a group of individual people or things, e.g. *audience, body, committee, government, team,* etc.

comparative   the form of an adjective or adverb ending in -*er* or preceded by more, e.g. *larger, happier, more safely*. See also **superlative**.

complement   a word or phrase that completes a sentence in some way, other than the subject, verb, and object, e.g. *librarian* in *They made her librarian* and *delighted* in *He is delighted*.

complex sentence   a sentence with a main clause and one or more subordinate clauses linked by a conjunction, e.g. *Read this article when you have a chance*.

compound sentence   a sentence with more than one main clause linked by a conjunction, e.g. *Read this article and tell me what you think of it*.

concrete noun   a noun that refers to a physical object, e.g. *ceiling, person, truck*. See also **abstract noun**.

conjunction   a word that links other words or groups of words, e.g. *and, but, if, unless, whether*.

consonant   any of the letters that are not vowels: *b, c, d, f, g, h, j, k, l, m, n, p, q, r, s, t, v, w, x, y* (e.g. in *yellow*), *z*.

countable noun   a noun that can form plurals, e.g. *bus, crisis, remark, kindness* = a kind act. See also **mass noun, uncountable noun**.

determiner   a word that comes before a noun and limits its meaning in some way, e.g. *a, the, this, some, each*, etc.

direct speech   speech that gives the actual words used, normally in quotation marks, e.g. *He said, 'You will be late.'* See also **indirect speech**.

ellipsis   the omission of certain words without loss of meaning, e.g. of *that* in the sentence *He told us [that] we would be late.*

finite   a finite form of a verb is one that is used in a particular tense, person, and number, e.g. *sat* in *They **sat** down* (as distinct from the base form *sit*).

future tense   the form of a verb that indicates an action or state still to come, e.g. *We **will be** there.*

future perfect tense   the form of a verb, typically formed with *shall have* or *will have*, that indicates an action or state that will be completed in relation to a point of time in the future, e.g. *By tomorrow they **will have** arrived.*

gender   a classification into masculine, feminine, and neuter. There is very little grammatical gender left in English, apart from the pronouns (*he*, *she*, *it*, *his*, *her*, etc.), some occupational nouns ending in *-ess* and *-ette*, and a few special nouns, e.g. *widow*, *widower*; *hero*, *heroine*.

gradable   a gradable adjective is one that can vary in intensity and be qualified by words such as *fairly*, *rather*, *very*, *more*, *less*, etc., e.g. *big*, *difficult*, *heavy*.

indirect question   a question put in a reported form (see **indirect speech** below), e.g. *He asked where the bathroom was, I wonder who that can be.*

indirect speech   speech in which the words used are reported by someone other than the original speaker, with a reporting verb such as *say, remark, tell,* etc., and with the tense and grammar of the words modified to suit this, e.g. *He told us we would be late.* See also **direct speech**.

infinitive the form of a word without any subject or inflection, e.g. *say* as distinct from *says* or *said*. An infinitive can either be unaccompanied (a bare infinitive, e.g. *I will say*) or be preceded by *to* (a *to*-infinitive, e.g. *I want to say*).

inflection the change in the forms of words to suit their role in the sentence, for example by adding *-s* to the third person singular of verbs (e.g. *comes, says*) or to form the plurals of nouns (e.g. *cakes, comments*) or by adding *-ed* or *-ing* to form the past or present participle.

interjection an exclamation such as *ah!, alas!, oops!*

interrogative an interrogative word or sentence is one that asks a question, e.g. *Are you ready?, Which car shall we take?*

intransitive an intransitive verb, or meaning of a verb, is one that does not have a grammatical object, e.g. *The door opened.* See also **transitive**.

main clause a part of a sentence, containing a verb, that makes complete sense by itself. See also **clause**.

main verb the verb in a main clause.

mass noun   a noun that is normally singular only, but unlike fully uncountable nouns can form plurals in the special sense 'an amount of', e.g. *beer* (*three beers*) or 'a type of', e.g. *cheese* (*try different cheeses*). See also **countable noun**, **uncountable noun**.

modal verbs   the verbs *can*, *could*, *may*, *might*, *must*, *shall*, *should*, *will*, and *would*, which are used to form moods (modes of expression denoting a fact, command, possibility, etc.) of other verbs. They can form negatives and questions without the help of *do*, they do not add *-s* in the third person singular, and they do not have an infinitive form.

modifier   a word, typically an adjective, that describes or modifies a noun in some way, e.g. *cold tea*, *coffee table*.

negative   a negative word or sentence denies that a fact is the case, typically by using words such as *no*, *not*, *never*, etc., or is equivalent to the answer 'no'. See also **affirmative**.

noun   a word that refers to a person or thing, e.g. *cat*, *health*, *sugar*, *Henry*, *Paris*. See also **abstract noun**, **concrete noun**, **proper noun**; **countable noun**, **mass noun**, **uncountable noun**; **collective noun**.

number   the grammatical categorization of nouns and other words as **singular** or **plural**.

object   the person or thing that is affected by the action of an active transitive verb, e.g. *Susan opened **the door**.*

objective the form of a word when it is the object of a verb or follows a preposition, especially of a pronoun, e.g. *me* and *her* instead of *I* and *she*. See also **subjective**.

part of speech a category based on the role that a word has in a sentence. The traditional parts of speech are noun, verb, adjective, adverb, pronoun, preposition, conjunction, and interjection.

participle see **past participle**, **present participle**.

passive the form of a verb in which the object of the action becomes the subject of the verb and the performer of the action is either not expressed or expressed after *by*, e.g. *The car was parked by her*. See also **active**.

past participle a form of a verb typically ending in *-ed* or *-t* (e.g. *danced*, *caught*) used to form past tenses and the passive voice.

past perfect (*or* pluperfect) tense a form of a verb, typically formed with *had*, denoting a state or action that is completed in relation to a point of reference in the past, e.g. *We had been waiting an hour when the bus finally came*.

past tense the form of a verb that indicates an action or state in the past, e.g. *We were there*.

perfect tense a form of a verb, typically formed with *have* or *has*, that refers to a past action or state in the context of the present, e.g. *I wonder if they have ever been to Paris*.

person a categorization of words according to whether the person or thing referred to is the speaker (first person, corresponding to the pronouns *I*, *me* and *we*), a person addressed (second person, corresponding to *you* singular or plural), or another person or thing (third person, corresponding to *he*, *she*, *it*, *they*, or a noun).

phrasal verb a combination of a verb and an adverb such as *off* and *up*, usually having a special meaning, e.g. *take off*, *give up*. An object of the verb can come between it and the adverb, e.g. *take your jacket off*.

phrase a group of words forming a grammatical unit but normally without a verb and not making complete sense by itself. A noun phrase (e.g. *the man in the moon*) is equivalent to a noun, an adverb phrase (e.g. *by the river*) is equivalent to an adverb, and so on.

plural a form of a noun, pronoun, or verb that refers to more than one individual, e.g. *cats*, *crises*, *people*. See also **singular**.

postpositive a modifier that comes after the noun it qualifies, e.g. *president* **elect**, *money* **galore**.

predicate the part of a sentence other than the subject, typically including a verb, object, and any adverb phrases, e.g. *The man* **took a note out of his wallet**.

predicative a predicative adjective is one that is placed in the predicate of a sentence, typically after the verb, e.g. *The door is* **red** as distinct from *the* **red** *door*. See also **attributive**.

preposition   a word that shows position in relation to space or time, e.g. *after* as in *after dinner, in, on, to, with,* etc.

present participle   a form of a verb ending in *-ing* (e.g. *dancing, catching*) used to form continuous tenses and verbal adjectives (e.g. *annoying, surprising*).

present tense   the form of a verb that refers to present time, e.g. *We* **are** *here.*

pronoun   a word that is used in place of a noun: *he, she, it, they, this, those,* etc.

proper noun   a noun that refers to a particular individual, e.g. *Everest, New York, Concorde.* The term is sometimes extended to include personal names, e.g. *David, Rebecca.*

quantifier   a type of modifier that indicates quantity, e.g. *some, a few, many,* etc.

reflexive   a word that refers back to the subject of the clause in which it occurs, typically ending in *-self* or *-selves,* e.g. *myself, yourself, herself, himself, itself, oneself, ourselves, yourselves, themselves.*

relative clause   a clause introduced by *that, which, who,* or *whose,* e.g. *The person* **who was here** *has gone; The animal* **that you saw** *was a goat.*

sentence   a group of words containing a main clause, typically with a verb, making complete sense by itself, and not linked grammatically to any larger structure.

sentence adverb   an adverb that qualifies a whole statement, e.g. **Clearly** *there had been a mistake.*

simple sentence a sentence consisting of a single main clause, e.g. *I am reading a book.* See also **complex sentence, compound sentence.**

singular a form of a noun, pronoun, or verb that refers to one individual (e.g. *cat, crisis, person*) or to the only form of an uncountable noun (e.g. *happiness, sugar*). See also **plural.**

split infinitive a *to*-infinitive in which a word, typically an adverb or adverb phrase, comes between *to* and the verb, e.g. *to really mean it.*

stress the part of a word that is emphasized more than the others, e.g. the first syllable in *matrimony* and the third in *matrimonial.*

subject the person or thing that performs the action of an active verb (e.g. ***Susan** opened the door*) or is affected by the action of a passive verb (e.g. ***The door** was opened by Susan*).

subjective the form of a word, especially of a pronoun, when it is the subject of a verb, e.g. *I* and *she.* See also **objective.**

subjunctive a special form of a verb, in English now limited to certain expressions of wish or command and usually noticeable only in the third person singular which does not end in *-s*, e.g. *God **save** the Queen*; ***perish** the thought.*

subordinate clause a clause that is not a main clause but is attached to the main clause of a sentence with a word such as *if, whether, who, which,* or *that.* See also **clause.**

superlative   the form of an adjective or adverb ending in *-est* or preceded by *most*, e.g. *largest, happiest, most safely*. See also **comparative**.

syllable   a unit of pronunciation that is uninterrupted and contains a vowel: there are three syllables in the word *hap-pi-ness*.

tense   the categorization of verbs according to whether the action or state is in the present, past, or future. See also **past tense, present tense, future tense**.

***that*-clause**   a clause introduced by *that*, e.g. *He knew **that I was wrong**. The word *that* can often be omitted, e.g. *He knew I was wrong*.

to*-infinitive**   an infinitive of a verb with the word *to* preceding it, e.g. *They wanted **to leave.

transitive   a transitive verb, or meaning of a verb, is one that has a grammatical object, e.g. *She **opened** the door*. See also **intransitive**.

uncountable noun   a noun that does not form a plural, e.g. *poverty, traffic, wealth*. See also **mass noun, countable noun**.

verb   a word that refers to an action (e.g. *go, lie, send*) or state (e.g. *be, exist, remain*).

verbal noun   a form of a verb ending in *-ing* used as a noun, e.g. ***dancing** is fun*.

vowel   any of the letters *a, e, i, o,* and *u*. The letter *y* is also classed as a vowel in words such as *rhythm and byte*.

wh- word   a word such as *who, what, which, when, where, why,* used to ask questions (e.g. ***Where** have you been?*) and to introduce subordinate clauses (e.g. *I don't know **what** you mean; They wanted to know **why** I had come*).

wordclass   another term for **part of speech**.

Further Reading

This is a list of books that will provide more general information about aspects of language (such as grammar, spelling, and punctuation) that are discussed in this book in more focused ways in the context of specific errors and problems. The list is in chronological order of publication:

Fowler, H. W. and F. G., *The King's English* (third edition, Oxford University Press, 1931: still in print and still a valuable guide, despite its age)

Blamires, Harry, *The Penguin Guide to Plain English* (Penguin Books, 2000)

Trask, R. L., *Mind the Gaffe: The Penguin Guide to Common Errors in English* (Penguin Books, 2001)

Cutts, Martin, *The Oxford Guide to Plain English* (second edition, Oxford University Press, 2004)

Seely, John, *Everyday Grammar* (Oxford University Press, 2004)

The New Oxford Dictionary for Writers and Editors (Oxford University Press, 2005: an alphabetical listing of words, phrases, and names that have problems of style or spelling or other special features)

Allen, Robert, *Pocket Fowler's Modern English Usage* (second edition, Oxford University Press, 2008: a modern version in shorter form of the classic book by H. W. Fowler)

There are also three relevant volumes in this series of Writers' Guides: my own *How to Write Better English*, and *Improve Your Spelling* and *How to Punctuate* (both by George Davidson).

It is important always to have a good up-to-date dictionary to hand: among the best (in order of publication) are the *Concise Oxford Dictionary* (revised eleventh edition, Oxford University Press, 2006), *The Chambers Dictionary* (tenth edition, Chambers, 2006), and the *Penguin English Dictionary* (third edition, Penguin Books, 2007).